THE PERSIAN WAR OF THE EMPEROR MAURICE
(582-602)

PART I. THE CHRONOLOGY, WITH A BRIEF HISTORY
OF THE PERSIAN CALENDAR

To Sister Marie Sigourie from Marten J. Higgins

THE CATHOLIC UNIVERSITY OF AMERICA
BYZANTINE STUDIES
VOL. I

"Let nothing disturb thee; All things pass away"

THE PERSIAN WAR OF THE
EMPEROR MAURICE
(582-602)

PART I. The Chronology, with a Brief History
of the Persian Calendar

A DISSERTATION

SUBMITTED TO THE FACULTY OF THE GRADUATE SCHOOL OF ARTS AND
SCIENCES OF THE CATHOLIC UNIVERSITY OF AMERICA IN PARTIAL
FULFILLMENT OF THE REQUIREMENTS FOR THE DEGREE OF
DOCTOR OF PHILOSOPHY

BY

REVEREND MARTIN J. HIGGINS
Priest of the Archdiocese of San Francisco

THE CATHOLIC UNIVERSITY OF AMERICA PRESS
WASHINGTON, D. C.
1939

PREFACE

The Emperor Maurice, the most prominent of the immediate successors of Justinian, is a personage of sufficient distinction to merit a special monograph. None exists, however, and a beginning is made here with a study of his Persian War. This study has been divided into three parts: Part I, the Chronology; Part II, The Sources; Part III, the Narrative of Events. Parts II and III are ready for publication, but as the whole work would be too bulky for a single volume, Part I is herewith published separately.

That a review of the accepted chronology was needed has long been felt and is proved by the present work. Into the *Chronological Table* which sums up its conclusions, only one of the relevant dates given by Dölger's *Regesten* can be admitted.

Almost all the changes result from the correction of a single item, the accession of the Persian king Chosroes II. Once this is accurately dated, the other events can be fitted into a consistent chronology. It owes its importance to an intimate connection with the crucial occurrence of the Persian War. Shortly after his coronation Chosroes was driven out by the usurper Bahram VI and fled to Maurice for protection. The prolonged conflict took thus a sudden and dramatic turn. It happens that the Greek historian Theophylactus Simocatta recounts the episode with considerable minuteness. To his narrative numerous circumstances can be added from other sources, chiefly Oriental, but it becomes impossible to adjust all the details properly if the central point is out of position. Hence, the whole of Chapter I is devoted to fixing the accession of Chosroes II accurately. The contents of the chapter are undeniably far removed from the Persian War of Maurice, but under the circumstances cannot be excluded.

Around the date for Chosroes' accession the rest of the chronology is built. Chapter II treats the circumstances leading up to this event, beginning in 588 with the Turkish invasion and the contemporaneous mutiny of the Roman troops. Chapter III discusses the aftermath of Chosroes' flight to his restoration in 591. This has been judged the most convenient place to dispose of the arguments of Nöldeke and Bury for the received date of Chosroes' accession.

Chapter IV takes up the period from 582 to 588. The principal fact established is that 585 was the year of the battle of Solachon, not 586.

An effort has been made to examine thoroughly all the Oriental sources of significance and to evaluate the data they contain. The criterion of reliability is Theophylactus Simocatta. Everything that fits into the frame of his narrative has been incorporated in the Chronology; whatever does not, has been rejected. It is amazing to find how much information is thus added. This is particularly true of the complex of writers who record the traditional history of Persia, the Persian and Arabic authors who drew on the *Khva-dhaynamagh* (Official Royal Annals). They have been to some extent rehabilitated. On the other hand, the *Anonymous of Four-mont* has not been employed. Besides being of no importance for the chronology, it is objectionable on grounds that will be explained at length in Part II. In brief they are as follows. Fourmont pretends to give the gist of a Turkish manuscript and insinuates that it derives from a Persian original. But his report includes many details so alien to the traditional history of Persia that they must come from a Greek source. That these have not been intruded by Fourmont himself is difficult to believe. Hence the *Anonymous* has been ignored.

The use of Oriental sources presents a special problem to any student unacquainted with the languages in which they are written. For the present treatise, all the translated sources have of course been consulted. Of the untranslated sources, it has been judged necessary to control only the *ex professo* historical writers previous to Firdausi. The Reverend Edward P. Arbez, S. S., S. T. D., Assistant Professor in the Department of Semitic and Egyptian Languages and Literatures at the Catholic University of America, has supplied versions of Ibn Qutaiba, Yaqubi, and Dinawari. These will be published as an appendix to the forthcoming Part II, The Sources.

The author wishes in the first place to express his heartfelt gratitude to His Excellency, the Most Reverend John J. Mitty, D. D., Archbishop of San Francisco, for the opportunity to pursue graduate studies and for his generous aid and encouragement. He thanks Professor Ernst Stein, Ph. D., formerly Professor of Byzantine

History at the Catholic University of America and now Professor
of Byzantine History at the University of Louvain, for introducing
him to Byzantine studies and suggesting the topic of the dissertation. He feels under the deepest obligation to Martin R. P.
McGuire, Ph. D., Associate Professor of Latin and Greek and Dean
of the Graduate School of Arts and Sciences of the Catholic University of America, for his direction of the whole work. He ac-
knowledges with pleasure his special indebtedness to the Reverend
Edward P. Arbez, S. S., S. T. D., for his kindness in translating
Ibn Qutaiba, Yaqubi, and Dinawari, as also for his careful reading
of the manuscript. He appreciates warmly the judicious criticisms
of the Reverend Aloysius K. Ziegler, S. T. D., *Archiviste-Paléo-
graphe,* who went over the whole work meticulously. He is grateful
to the Reverend Professor Adolphe A. Vaschalde, Ph. D., and to the
Reverend Patrick W. Skehan, S. T. D., for helpful suggestions, and
to Sister M. Inviolata Barry, C. D. P., Ph. D., Our Lady of the Lake
College, San Antonio, Texas, for aid in preparing the manuscript
for the printer. Finally, the author pays his tribute of gratitude
and esteem to Professor Roy J. Deferrari, Ph. D., Head of the
Department of Greek and Latin, and to the Right Reverend Monsignor Henri Hyvernat, P. A., O. ⚜, S. T. D., Litt. D., Head of the
Department of Semitic and Egyptian Languages and Literatures.
Without the splendid library of the Foundation for Research in
Christian Oriental Literature, for which Monsignor Hyvernat is
primarily responsible, the present work would have been impossible.

St. Patrick's Day, 1939

TABLE OF CONTENTS

CHAPTER I

Brief History of the Persian Calendar Under the Sassanids

The most intricate problem in the chronology of the Persian war of the Emperor Maurice is to determine the accession of the contemporary Persian king Chosroes II. Theophylactus Simocatta puts it in the spring of 590. An inscription set up by Chosroes himself implies—at least in its obvious interpretation—that the event could not have occurred before June 27, 590. The latter has been deemed decisive by modern scholarship; that, on the contrary, the former is fully as authoritative, is demonstrated in the present discussion of the Persian calendar. The argument here advanced concerns directly the date of the coronation of Bahram. It is shown that his usurpation of the throne of Persia, which was subsequent to the accession of Chosroes II, occurred long before June 27, 590. The connection between the Persian calendar and the coronation of Bahram arises from a purely fortuitous circumstance. The date given for the event by Theophylactus and a Persian epic poet Firdausi, by providing a synchronism of the Persian with the Julian year, leads to deductions about the Sassanid calendar the accuracy of which can readily be tested. Thus is established the reliability of Theophylactus' date.

Preliminary to the study of his text, it is necessary to understand the detailed arrangement of the Persian calendar.[1] The Persians

[1] A. von Gutschmid, "Über das iranische Jahr," *Ber. üb. d. Verh. d. kgl. sächs. Ges. d. Wiss., phil.-hist. Cl.*, 14 (1862) 1-9; A. D. Mordtmann, "Hekatompylos. Ein Beitrag zur vergleichenden Geographie Persiens," *Sitzungsber. bayer. Akad.*, 1869, Part I, pp. 497-536, esp. 503 f.; *id.*, "Die Chronologie der Sassaniden," *Sitzungsber. bayer. Akad.*, 1 (1871) 3-30; Th. Nöldeke, *Geschichte der Perser und Araber zur Zeit der Sasaniden, aus der arabischen Chronik des* Tabari *übersetzt und mit ausführlichen Erläuterungen und Ergänzungen versehn* (Leiden 1879), pp. 403-7; F. K. Ginzel, *Handbuch der mathematischen und technischen Chronologie* (Leipzig 1906-14), I 275-309; D. Hans Lietzmann, *Zeitrechnung der römischen Kaiserzeit, des Mittelalters und der Neuzeit für die Jahre 1-2000 nach Christus* (Berlin and Leipzig 1934), (*Sammlung Göschen Nr. 1085*);

1

of Sassanid times had what is known as a vague year, that is, an inexact solar year of always 365 days, which, because no allowance is made for a leap year, is said to " wander " through the whole fixed year. For example, if the beginning of the Persian year corresponded to January 1, 4 A. D., the next Persian year would begin December 31, 4 A. D., and January 1, 5 A. D. would coincide with the second day of the Persian year. In other words, for every four years, the Persian calendar would advance one day on the Julian. As for further distinctive features, it comprised twelve months of exactly thirty days each with five epagomenae (additional days belonging to no month). Moreover, in the Julian calendar the days of the week are named and the days of the month numbered; in the Persian numbers were not used, every day of the month having a name of its own. Thus the Persian spoke not of Wednesday the first and Saturday the eleventh, but of the day Ormuzd and the day Khur, respectively, of such or such a month.[2] This was the calendar in everyday use, the civil calendar, serving precisely the

Arthur Christensen, *L'Iran sous les Sassanides* (Copenhagen 1936), pp. 163-72; S. H. Taqizadeh, " Some Chronological Data relating to the Sasanian Period," *Bull. of the School of Or. Stud. (Univ. of London)*, 9 (1937) 125-39.

Von Gutschmid's basic article rendered all previous studies obsolete and for the first time correctly explained the arrangement of the Persian calendar. Mordtmann's distinct contribution was his use of the numismatic evidence for fixing the chronology of the Sassanids. Nöldeke, pp. 405, n. 1; 407, determined the proper method both of calculating the beginning of the Persian civil year and of counting the regnal years of the Sassanid kings; in *Anhang A*, p. 435, he summarizes the now generally undisputed chronology of the Sassanids, and in *Anhang B*, p. 436, he draws up a table of the Persian New Year's Day from 224 to 652. Taqizadeh's important contribution will be fully explained later, and Ginzel's standard work needs no description here. Christensen has been cited for his excellent account of the religious feasts and because his is the most recent treatment of the subject; both in him and in Ginzel the reader will find additional bibliography. Ginzel, pp. 290-93, has also a translation of the principal sources. Lietzmann's booklet, though it does not deal with the Persian calendar, is mentioned here because it has nevertheless proved very useful throughout the present work.

[2] For the names and order of the Persian months, see the *Persian Calendar, infra.* p. 23. In this table the Persian names of the days are not used, but, for greater convenience, the days have been numbered.

purposes that the Gregorian does for western civilization; it was employed for all ordinary business public or private, for the laws of the king, for contracts, for personal correspondence.

The Persians, however, felt this calendar quite unsuitable for dating their religious feasts. Such observances had been originally bound up with the seasons, but, obviously, the relation was lost by the vague year. In his brilliant article [3] von Gutschmid showed how the Zoroastrian clergy invented a remedy for this inconvenience. Alongside the civil was set up a religious year, whose sole and exclusive purpose was to date the various sacred acts and functions. This "ecclesiastical" calendar differed only in being fixed, not vague. It was adjusted to the spring equinox, not by the insertion of a day every four years, but by the intercalation of a month every 120 years. In every other respect both calendars were exactly alike; they had the same arrangement of days and months and the same names for both.

By devising an ingenious system of inserting the extra month, the clergy brought the fixed religious calendar into constant relation with the vague civil year. The intercalated month was placed after the last month Esfendarmuz of the fixed year and its name was always taken from the month of the civil calendar that happened to run concurrently. The epagomenae were transferred to the end of this month of the civil calendar and their position marked the following month of the civil year as the beginning of the religious year. An example will make this clear. Presumably, the epagomenae originally stood at the end of the year after the last month Esfendarmuz. Thus, if the year of the institution of the cycle is called the year 1, the two calendars would run exactly parallel until the year 121; both would then begin thirty days ahead of the spring equinox. The calendars for the years 120-21 would be as follows:

Year 120 (civil)   Year 120 (religious)
  1. Ferverdin   1. Ferverdin
12. Esfendarmuz   12. Esfendarmuz
       Epagomenae omitted

---

[3] Esp. pp. 7-9.

Year 121

1. Ferverdin ....13. Ferverdin II
   Epagomenae   Epagomenae
                        Year 121
2. Urdi Behesht   1. Ferverdin

The system can be seen from the above scheme. The civil year 120 continues on into 121 as usual, with the exception that the epagomenae are omitted after Esfendarmuz, where they stood for the first 120 years, and transferred to the end of Ferverdin. In the religious calendar, however, the beginning of the year 121 has to be postponed for thirty days in order to make it fall once again on the spring equinox. Consequently, in the year 120 a thirteenth month is inserted, which takes its name from the concurrent month of the civil calendar, Ferverdin. This Ferverdin is the *first* month of the *new* year in the civil calendar, but the *thirteenth* month of the *old* year in the religious calendar. It comes twice, therefore, in the religious year 120, whence the name, Ferverdin II. In the civil year for the next 120 years the epagomenae remain attached to Ferverdin. Urdi Behesht, now preceded by the epagomenae, is thereby marked as concurrent with Ferverdin of the religious year and is the month of spring.

Another example will make the device clearer:

Year 241 (civil)   Year 240 (religious)
1. Ferverdin   12. Esfendarmuz
        Epagomenae omitted
2. Urdi Behesht.............13. Urdi Behesht II
   Epagomenae   Epagomenae
                        Year 241
3. Khurdad   1. Ferverdin

In the second return of the cycle of 120 years when the religious year 241 is postponed for thirty days, Urdi Behesht is the concurrent month of the civil year. It becomes the thirteenth and leap month of the religious year 240 and carries the epagomenae, while Khurdad is the spring month that corresponds to Ferverdin of the religious year. In this fashion the epagomenae fell back successively behind each month of the civil year and their position always marked the month immediately following them as concurrent with Ferverdin of the religious year. By 590 A. D. they had come to the end of the eighth month Aban. Then the first day of the ninth month Azur coincided with the first of Ferverdin in the religious calendar.[4]

By this peculiar type of adjustment the Zoroastrians achieved several purposes of the highest importance to themselves. First of all, the transference of the epagomenae was essential to the proper celebration of the *Nauruz*.[5] The *Nau-ruz* (New-Day) proper corresponded to New Year's Day. It was the day Ormuzd of the month Ferverdin—the first day of the first month. The religious observance, however, began with the epagomenae, which were devoted to the remembrance of the dead and always very closely bound up with the *Nauruz*. Moreover, the festivities included not only the New Year's Day itself but the following five days and culminated in the *Great Nauruz*, the day Khurdad—the sixth—of the month Ferverdin. The epagomenae and the *Nauruz* formed a group so intimately connected that they received the collective name *Ferverdigan* (other forms are *Fravardighan, Frordighan*). If this whole complex of eleven days was to be maintained in its integrity, the epagomenae had to remain constantly at the beginning of the fixed religious year. Just, however, as the vague year advanced in relation to the fixed year, the civil calendar advanced on the epagomenae. This is a much more exact statement of the result than to say that the epagomenae fell back successively in the civil year. In any event, the apparent shift of the epagomenae was a very simple and ingenious device to mark the relation of the vague civil calendar to the spring equinox.

The management of the epagomenae was probably only subordinate to another end that the Zoroastrians had in view. A glance at the *Persian Calendar* will show that, though the months in each calendar were different, the names of the days were always the

---

[4] Von Gutschmid, p. 3; Ginzel, pp. 287. 291. 293. 296. 298-99; Christensen, p. 165.

[5] Von Gutschmid, pp. 6 f. 9; Ginzel, pp. 287. 288. 294; Christensen, pp. 165. 166 f. Nöldeke, p. 407, n. 2, suggests that the term *Nauruz* be confined to the festival, and New Year's Day to the beginning of the civil year.

2

same.[6]   This parallelism was designed; it was almost a necessity. If the epagomenae, for instance, in each calendar had failed to correspond, it would no doubt have occasioned as great inconvenience as if the Sunday of the modern ecclesiastical year with its laws for public worship and cessation from labor were a different day from that of the civil week.   But, apart from this obvious advantage, the Zoroastrians had quite another reason for keeping the parallelism inviolate.   For the order of the days they had a superstitious awe. It was indispensable that rites be accomplished on the proper day. An act of worship performed on the wrong day was deemed invalid, and any dislocation in the succession of days nullified the religious proceedings throughout.   It was, consequently, intolerable to the Zoroastrians to have an adjustment similar to the modern leap year; for them the only possible intercalary unit was the month.[7]   In fact, the conjecture may be hazarded that the inviolability of the order of days provided the dominant motive in the whole system of adjustment of the civil and the religious calendar.   Apparently the months had no particular significance from this standpoint.   The only exception was the first month Ferverdin, whose intimate relation to the epagomenae has just been described.   The principal problem was to make the epagomenae concurrent in both the civil and the religious year.   Since these additional days constituted practically a thirteenth unit of the calendar, they lent themselves readily enough to a device whereby they were fixed to the religious year and became a sort of pivot for the revolving vague year.   Once this solution was hit upon, the complete parallelism of the days throughout both calendars followed automatically.

The above theory has been proved beyond any doubt by Taqizadeh.[8]   He cites the following passage from the Pahlavi book, *Selections of Zadsparam*: "In the forty-seventh year died Zaratusht, who was aged seventy-seven years, forty days, in the month Urdi

---

[6] *Infra*, p. 23.   As stated above, numbers have been substituted in this table for the Persian names of the days.

[7] The source of this statement is Albiruni; cf. *The Chronology of Ancient Nations, an English Version of . . . Albiruni . . .* by E. Sachau (London 1879), p. 54.   The translation in Ginzel's *Handbuch*, p. 292, does not seem in this instance to be quite clear.

[8] In the article referred to above, p. 2, n. 1.

Behesht,[9] on the day Khur. By eight months *vihezhakik* it has been carried to the month Dei and the day Khur, which *vihezhakik* month is the same month Urdi Behesht." [10] The meaning of the excerpt is obvious. There were two calendars, one of which, the fixed, according to Taqizadeh, was called *vihezhakik*. In this fixed religious calendar was kept the real anniversary of Zoroaster's death, the eleventh day (Khur) of the month Urdi Behesht; the movable year, however, had advanced eight months at the date of writing with the result that the eleventh of Dei, civil calendar, corresponded to the eleventh of Urdi Behesht, religious calendar. In this passage, then, explicit mention is made not only of a double calendar but also of the dates in both that corresponded, and the evidence agrees precisely with what should be expected on von Gutschmid's theory.[11] He [12] bases his view on the descriptions of later Arabic writers, citing no actual example from the sources to support it. Consequently, the unmistakable confirmation supplied by Zadsparam is of the utmost importance.[13]

There is one feature of the quotation from Zadsparam that must be emphasized: the *day* is the same in both the civil and the religious calendar. Taqizadeh does not direct any special attention to this, but it is of capital importance for the conclusion presently to be drawn. As von Gutschmid conjectured,[14] the months differ. Dei in the one corresponds to Urdi Behesht in the other; but it is the same eleventh day, Khur, in both.

The above account summarizes the present information on the arrangement of the Persian calendar. The texts of Theophylactus and Firdausi now come up for scrutiny.

<hr>

[9] For the sake of consistency, the liberty has been taken of substituting in this quotation the less scientifically transcribed forms of the day- and month-names used everywhere in this dissertation.

[10] P. 132.

[11] The truth of this can be seen clearly from the *Persian Calendar, infra,* p. 23.

[12] Pp. 2 f.

[13] For Zadsparam, cf. E. W. West, *Pahlavi Literature (Grundriss der iranischen Philologie,* Strasbourg 1895 ff.), II 104. The late date of this author (890) is, of course, no objection to his authority as he followed the Era of Yezdegerd. For this *vide infra,* pp. 14 f.

[14] P. 9.

Theophylactus, first of all, makes it clear that the coronation of Bahram took place in spring, long before June 27, 590. Beginning his narrative of Bahram's defeat by Romanus he gives the date, the eighth year of Maurice, August 14, 589-90.[15] He then relates how the Persian general revolted, moved down out of Azerbaijan and took up a position on the Zab. Again, he marks the time: winter had now set in.[16] Proceeding with his story, he details the dispersal of Hormisdas' last army, the consequent deposition of that monarch and the *coup d'état* that brought his son, Chosroes II, to the throne. Thereupon, Bahram had marched upon Ctesiphon and himself taken the crown. Forced to flee, Chosroes in all haste sought refuge with the Romans and immediately sent ambassadors to Maurice to ask aid. At this moment the source again indicates the season: it was at the beginning of spring that the appeal was dispatched.[17] Theophylactus gives even more exact information. The throne had been usurped a little more than seven days after the precipitate departure of Chosroes [18] and some short time before that monarch reached Hierapolis, where he wrote his request to the Emperor.[19] No exception can possibly be taken to this chronology; it is perfectly logical, clear, and consistent. The narrative is minute and circumstantial and the passage of time is marked with the utmost accuracy. From the variety and precision of the references it is manifest that Bahram's coronation took place either just at, or just before, the start of spring.

Theophylactus says more specifically that it occurred "on the great and famous festival which an ancient and time-honored law decreed that the Persians solemnize to the Sky." [20] He makes an unmistakable reference here to the celebration of the *Nauruz*. In the first place, he puts the event "at the beginning of spring"—a formula by which he also refers elsewhere to the *Nauruz*. As in both instances the feast actually came at the end of winter, the choice of expression seems to have been influenced by the Persian point of view.[21] Further, not only was the *Nauruz* a spring festival, it was the greatest festival of the Persian year. As has just been

[15] *Theophylacti Simocattae historiae*, ed. by C. de Boor (Leipzig 1887), III 6, 7.

[16] IV 2, 1. [18] IV 12, 2. [20] IV 12, 6.
[17] IV 13, 3. [19] IV 12, 6-8. [21] *Infra*, p. 25.

mentioned, it lasted for eleven days. During the holiday all work ceased. Particularly the period from the *Nauruz* to the *Great Nauruz* (the first to the sixth Ferverdin) was a season of the utmost joy enlivened by every sort of popular ceremony and climaxed on the *Great Nauruz* by the exchange of gifts.[22] There was, in fact, no solemnity of the whole Sassanid calendar that could be more readily characterized as "*the* great and famous festival." Again, the deity honored above all others thus at the opening of the year was Ormuzd (Ahura Mazda) who was the Highest God, the creator of man and the renewer of life. Him Theophylactus identifies with the Sky by a learned reminiscence of a well-known passage of Herodotus.[23] Finally, it was an ancient custom for a king to assume the throne publicly and solemnly on the *Nauruz*.[24] It was undoubtedly, therefore, in the course of the *Nauruz* that Bahram VI took the crown.

By a happy chance the exact date also of this event according to the civil calendar is preserved in the *Shahname* of Firdausi.[25] The poet tells of how Bahram, after a stormy session with the nobles,[26] drew up a declaration which set forth the legitimacy of his claim to the throne. An unquiet night passed, the epic goes on, and early on the next day the usurper "placed upon his head the crown of the Keyanids (Achaemenids)." He now brought out the document; all the grandees signed it and recognized him as king of the world. "This took place in the month Azur and on the day Khur."[27] He then proclaimed that all who disagreed with what

[22] Christensen, *L'Iran*, pp. 166 f.; cf. *id.*, *Les types du premier homme et du premier roi dans l'histoire légendaire des Iraniens* II (Leiden 1934) 146-50.

[23] I 131. The passage has been much discussed; cf., for instance, the article "Mazdaismus" in *RE* SB V 691 f. (Clemen).

[24] Christensen, *L'Iran*, p. 175, n. 1.

[25] *Le livre des rois par Aboulkasim Firdousi traduit et commenté par* Jules Mohl (Paris 1876-78), VII 63.

[26] VII 56-63.

[27] The day Khur is the eleventh day of the month. Nöldeke, *Tab.*, p. 282, n. 2, however, in referring to this passage, speaks of the tenth, not the eleventh. This is an oversight. Rev. Edward P. Arbez, S. S., S. T. D., of the Department of Semitic and Egyptian Languages and Literatures of the Catholic University of America has been kind enough to verify the text of

he had done must leave the realm within three days or suffer death. The day Khur of the Month Azur corresponds to March 9 in the Julian calendar; this was, therefore, the coronation day.[28]

By combining the data from both Theophylactus and Firdausi, considerable information may be gained about the Persian calendar. In 590 the *Nauruz*, a festival celebrated in Ferverdin of the religious calendar, took place in the month Azur of the civil year. This correspondence agrees precisely with von Gutschmid's theory and offers a striking confirmation of it. As, however, his views seem to be received without question by modern scholars, there is no need to insist here on proving them further.[29] Their correctness may be taken for granted. But, in addition to the fact that Ferverdin parallels Azur, the days in the respective months ought to be exactly the same. They are not. The very use of the term *Frordighan* (*Ferverdigan*) shows the inseparability of the epagomenae from the first five days of the religious calendar;[30] and the *Great Nauruz*, coming as it did immediately afterwards and climaxing the feast, could not occur later than Ferverdin 6. Yet, the day Khur is the eleventh day. Therefore, in 590 the *Great Nauruz* must have been celebrated on Azur 11, the whole festival must have taken place Azur 6-11, and these days of the civil calendar must have corresponded with Ferverdin 1-6 of the religious calendar. The only possible conclusion is that the civil year had gotten five days ahead of the religious.

The explanation for this anomaly is obvious. The epagomenae

Firdausi in Turner Macan's *The Shah Nameh . . . by Abool Kasim Firdousee . . .* (Calcutta 1829), IV 1901, line 2. It reads: بازر مه روز هور . . . (b'adhrmah . . . ruz hor). *Hor* is but a collateral form of *Khur* from the same root; cf. Paul Horn, *Neupersische Schriftsprache* (*Grundr. d. iran Philol.*), Vol. I, Part IV, pp. 36, 38. Cf. also the translation of Arthur George Warner and Edmond Warner, *The Shahnama of Firdausi done into English* (London 1905-25), VIII 244, who translate: " 'Twas on the day Khurshid of month Azar." (*Khurshid* is another name of *Khur*.)

[28] See the *Persian Calendar*, *infra*, p. 23. This will aid the reader in following the complicated changes of 590.

[29] For instance, Christensen, *L'Iran*, p. 166, takes this theory for granted and mentions no other.

[30] *Supra*, p. 5.

had been suppressed in the civil but maintained in the religious calendar. The reason was probably the following. Theophylactus gives a very minute narrative of the interval between the coronation of Chosroes II and of Bahram VI, indicating the time practically day by day. An analysis of the details shows it was precisely during the epagomenae that the two rivals faced each other on the banks of the Naharwan.[31] The intercalary days were regarded by the Persians as of very ill omen.[32] On the *Nauruz* itself the "King abstained from discussing any matter, fearing lest something unpleasant should come of it and head the whole year."[33] Menander gives a very interesting illustration of this superstition of the Persians and shows that it existed in all its strength at the end of the sixth century.[34] He relates that the Roman envoy of Justin II could not even enter Persian territory until the *Frordighan* was over. The *Frordighan* was, therefore, the most unpropitious moment possible for anyone to inaugurate a critical struggle, and the epagomenae were probably omitted by mutual consent. On the other hand, it may be surmised that the *Frordighan* was too sacred to be entirely neglected in any year, and that a compromise was reached. It was observed in the religious, and disregarded only in the civil year.

The consequences of this singular phenomenon cannot be appreciated until another feature of the Persian calendar is determined: the several dates at which the epagomenae were shifted. These are easily calculated from the synchronism, Ferverdin 6 of the religious year equals March 9 in 590. In the readjustment of the calendar to the solar year the immediate aim was to keep the *Nauruz* in spring;[35] but the question arises: What day precisely was made to coincide with the equinox? So long as the solution of this problem depended upon *a priori* considerations, good arguments could be

---

[31] *Infra*, p. 30.   [32] Ginzel, p. 171.

[33] R. Ehrlich, "The Celebration and Gifts of the Persian New Year (Nawruz) according to an Arabic Source, Translated from the Arabic," *Dr. Modi Memorial Volume* (Bombay 1930), p. 98.

[34] *Excerpta de legationibus Romanorum ad gentes edidit* C. de Boor (*Excerpta historica iussu imp. Constantini Porphyrogeniti confecta*, Berlin 1903-10), I 189, lines 9-11.

[35] *Supra*, p. 3.

advanced for Ferverdin 1, for Ferverdin 6, or, as assumed by von Gutschmid,[36] for Ferverdin 19.

The above synchronism does away with all such doubts if first the time is discovered at which the previous intercalation occurred. Some Arabic authors place it under Chosroes I (531-79).[37] Albiruni, however, says that the fixed calendar was corrected for the last time in the reign of Yezdegerd I (399-420) ; that two months were then inserted, not one; that, as a result, the epagomenae were transferred to the end of Aban and before Azur, where they remained until the destruction of the Sassanid dynasty made further rearrangement impossible.[38] This conflict of the sources is fortunately settled by a remark in the *Life of Grighor* that in Kawad's (488-531) thirtieth year (July 20, 517-18) the *Frordighan* fell in the month *Adhar*.[39] If the Persian Azur (Adhar is an earlier form of the name) is meant, it decides the question. Hoffmann, however, asserts that " it naturally refers to the Syrian month "[40] that corresponds to March in the Julian calendar. In 518, therefore, the *Frordighan* would have been celebrated in March. Now, as repeatedly stated, the epagomenae formed an integral part of the feast, and the *Naruz* was always the first day of the month which they preceded in the civil calendar. Let it be supposed that Chosroes I made the intercalation and shifted the extra days to the end of Aban. Then, in the reign of his predecessor, Kawad, they must have stood one month ahead at least, and the latest possible position is just before Aban. This brings the *Naruz* on Aban 1. That day fell on February 20 in 518, and it could come on March 1 at the latest in 483, five years before Kawad came to the

---

[36] P. 8; the choice was guided, possibly, by the fact that Ferverdin 19 was to fall on the spring equinox in the reformed calendar of Jalal-ad-Din (Ginzel, p. 300).

[37] Summarized in Ginzel, p. 291; cf. v. Gutschmid, pp. 3. 9, who prefers them to Albiruni.

[38] *Chron. of Anc. Nations*, p. 56, Sachau.

[39] Georg Hoffmann, *Auszüge aus syrischen Akten persischer Märtyrer übersetzt und durch Untersuchungen zur historischen Topographie erläutert* (*Abhandlungen für die Kunde des Morgenlandes, herausgegeben von der Deutschen Morgenländischen Gesellschaft, VII, Nr. 3,* Leipzig 1880), p. 79.

[40] *Ibid.*, n. 720.

throne.[41] Albiruni's reliability, therefore, may be accepted without hesitancy.

Now, according to him two months were intercalated on this occasion instead of one. How is this statement to be interpreted? It must mean that sometime between 399 and 420 a cycle of 120 years came to an end, and that the religious year was then not exactly equated with the solar but set a month behind it. In other words, the beginning of the fixed calendar, instead of being connected with the spring equinox, March 19,[42] was made to fall on April 18. With this information it is possible to determine the year in which the adjustment was made. It is known that in 590 Ferverdin 1 of the religious year was on March 4 and that the likely adjustment-days were the first, the sixth, and the nineteenth

[41] As Ginzel gives no formula for reducing Persian dates of the Sassanid Era, it may help the reader to have an example worked out here, the process being analogous to that used for the Mohammedan calendar by Lietzmann, pp. 8-11. 1. Find the number of days from January 1 to the Persian New Year's; 2. Add the number of days elapsed of the Persian year to the given date, allowing always for the position of the epagomenae; 3. The answer gives the number of days from the January 1 of the year in which the Persian New Year's occurred to the given date: if it be less than 365 (or, in a leap year, 366), e. g., 290, find the 291st day of the year; if it be more, subtract 365 (or 366) and find the corresponding day in the following year. Thus, to find Aban 1 in Kawad's thirtieth year. The New Year's was July 20, 517 = 200 (Lietzmann has handy tables for this, pp. 102 f.). Aban 1 (first day of the eighth month, and the epagomenae are assumed in the text to have preceded it) = 7 × 30 + 5 (do not count in Aban 1 itself) = 215. 200 + 215 = 415 — 365 = 50 = February 20 of the following year, i. e., 518. The other date mentioned in the text may be found by working backward: March-1 = 59 + 365 = 424 — 215 = 209 = July 29. This was the New Year's of 480-83. The reader must be careful always to take one day less than the actual number of the given date; e. g., for Ferverdin 17, count only 16 days of Ferverdin, because, though Ferverdin 17 is the seventeenth day of the year, it is only 16 days from 1 January to 17 January.

[42] Cf. Ginzel, p. 101. (Note that the table gives astronomical days from midday to midday and allow 2ʰ 58ᵐ for difference in time between Greenwich and Babylon.) The equinox fell on March 19.1625 in 400 A. D.; i. e., March 19, 6:52 P. M. at Babylon. As the Persians counted the day from sunrise to sunrise (*ibid.*, p. 288), they would reckon the equinox for March 19 throughout the period in question.

of the same month. The only one of these dates that fell on April 18 between 399 and 420 was Ferverdin 1, and that in 408.[43]

It is now easy to calculate the position of the epagomenae in the civil year for any period. They came to their position following Aban in 408. For the previous 120 years, 288-407, they stood, as has just been shown, at the end of the sixth month, Shehriver. From 168 to 287 they must be reckoned behind the fifth month, Murdad. The possibility cannot be ignored, however, that the Persian calendar was regulated more exactly than the Julian, which fell about a day behind the sun for every century. The Sassanid astronomers took fresh observations for each intercalation [44] and very likely inherited the accurate computations of the Babylonians and Egyptians, if not of the Greeks. They may, therefore, have inserted the leap months at intervals of 124 or 128 years. Practically, the small difference need not here be taken into account. It affects only the period, 280-88, and none of the dates discussed below fall within it.

The chronology of the shift of the epagomenae has now been determined. Before, however, studying the effect of their omission in 590, it is necessary to digress and explain the process by which the Persian New Year's Day [45] is calculated. The method is as follows. From the time that the Persians lost their independence to the Mohammedans in the caliphate of Omar (634-44) they used an era known as the Era of Yezdegerd. It began on June 16, 632.[46] In Sassanid times, however, they had no era, but reckoned only according to the years of the reigning monarch. As is customary wherever this system obtains, they made the regnal years concurrent with those of the calendar by counting them not from the accession but from the previous New Year's Day.[47] Chosroes I, for instance, ascended the throne on September 13, 531;[48] but he counted his first year from July 17, 531.[49] The last king of the Persians was Yezdegerd III. As he had no successor, the Persians

[43] Ferverdin 19 fell on April 18 in 480-81; Ferverdin 6 in 428-29.
[44] Albiruni, quoted in Ginzel's *Handb.*, I 292.
[45] Ferverdin 1 of the civil year; cf. *supra*, p. 5, n. 5.
[46] Ginzel, p. 298; Nöldeke, p. 407.
[47] Nöldeke, pp. 403 f.
[48] *Ibid.*, p. 435.   [49] See the *Table, infra*, p. 22.

were forced after his death to continue their reckoning by his regnal years. This is the origin of the Era of Yezdegerd. Its first day, June 16, 632, can be nothing but the beginning of the Persian year in the course of which he became king.[50] It has been pointed out above that the New Year's Day of the vague year advances one day for every four years of the Julian calendar.[51] Since the New Year's Day was June 16 in 632, it was June 17, a day later, in 628 and June 15, a day earlier, in 636. It was on this principle that Nöldeke drew up his table of the Persian New Year's Day.[52] Its correctness from 592 to 652 is conclusively proved by the correspondence in the dates given in terms of both Persian and Julian calendars for the death of Chosroes II.[53]

But the omission of the epagomenae in 590 obviously necessitates a revision of Nöldeke's table for all years previous to that date. The Persian civil year 589-90 had not 365, but only 360 days. The New Year's Day of 590, calculated back from June 16, 632, fell on June 27, 590. But the New Year's Day of 589 preceded June 27 by only 360 days and, calculated back from June 27, fell on July 2. This date provides a new point of departure from which the New Year's dates previous to 589 must be determined. They will be found in the *Revised Table of the Persian New Year's Day.*[54] That this table, and not Nöldeke's, is correct, is proven by the following considerations.

1. The Armenian Era. The Armenian Era began on July 11, 552, and, as the calendar is modeled very closely on the Persian, ran for centuries alongside the Era of Yezdegerd, with the odd difference that it always remained five days behind.[55] While von Gutschmid and Nöldeke conjectured that the discrepancy had resulted from some confusion in the epagomenae,[56] nevertheless, because they both regarded July 6 as the start of the Persian civil year, 552-53, they had, of course, no means of knowing just when or how the peculiarity arose. The omission of the five extra days in 590 offers a satisfactory explanation. The New Year's Day of 552 is thus

[50] Ginzel, p. 298; Nöldeke, p. 407.
[51] *Supra*, p. 2. [53] *Ibid.*, p. 407.
[52] P. 436. [54] *Infra*, p. 22.
[55] Ginzel, III 314-21; v. Gutschmid, p. 4; Nöldeke, p. 406, n. 4.
[56] Nöldeke, *ibid.*; v. Gutschmid, p. 9.

brought down to July 11, the precise day from which Armenia counted its Era. In 590, however, almost all of the country passed from the Persians to the Romans,[57] and, not being subject to the decree suppressing the epagomenae, naturally kept the normal year. In 590, therefore, the Persians began their year on June 27, but the Armenians on July 2. Thus originated the difference. The calendars were never brought into uniformity, because the two peoples that used them were not henceforth reunited in a bond sufficiently intimate and sufficiently lasting to make the disagreement a matter of inconvenience to either.

2. The date of Mani's death. One of the recently discovered documents pertaining to Manichaeism sets the death of Mani on Monday, Shehriver 4, at eleven o'clock, but without mention of the year,[58] while another, composed in 795, states that it occurred 522 years before the time of writing, i. e., in 273.[59] Schaeder derived February 14, 276 from Shehriver 4 by the following reasoning: it is known that Mani was executed by Bahram I (273-76); Shehriver 4 fell on February 14 from 272 to 276, but on a Monday only in 276.[60] He has no explanation for the other document's 273.[61] Taqizadeh, working independently, came to the same conclusion.[62] The calculation is open to the objection that it neglects the shift of the epagomenae, quite apart from the fact that it assumes September 14 as the New Year's Day (Nöldeke's).[63] The hypothesis has

[57] *Infra*, p. 39.

[58] W. Henning, " Mitteliranische Manichaica aus Chinesisch-Turkestan III. von F. C. Andreas (†), aus dem Nachlass herausgegeben," *Sitzungsber. Berl. Akad., philos.-hist. Kl.* (1934), pp. 861. 864. One of these documents, composed 110 years after the death of Mani (pp. 864 f.), i. e., 383, is naturally of great weight.

[59] A. von le Coq, " Türkische Manichaica aus Chotscho," *Abh. Berl. Akad., philos.-hist. Kl.* (1911), p. 39, n. 16 (to the document on pp. 11 f.).

[60] Cf. " Carl Schmidt und H. J. Polotsky: Ein Mani-Fund . . . ," *Gnomon*, 9 (1933) 351 and n. 4.

[61] He presumes that, as the era normally used among the Manichaeans dated from the founder's birth, the figure 522 must represent a calculation— and a mistaken one; cf. " Iranica," *Abh. Gött., philol.-hist. Kl.*, III. Folge, Nr. 10 (1934), pp. 79 f., n. 4.

[62] P. 126.

[63] Nöldeke's New Year's of 272, September 14 = 257. Shehriver 4 = 5 × 30 + 3 = 153 + 257 — 366 = 44 = February 14. Nöldeke, p. 411, n. 2, takes

been advanced above that the New Year's Day was five days later, September 19, and that the epagomenae preceded Shehriver from 168 to 288. By figuring anew on this basis, February 24 is obtained as coinciding with Shehriver 4 from 272 to 276, and February 24 fell on a Monday in 273. This brings the two documents into agreement and confirms the conclusions of this dissertation.[64]

3. The Chronology of the Syriac Acts of the Persian Martyrs.[65] In these Acts two systems of dating are followed: [66] the familiar Syriac method that began the year with First-Teshri (October) 1 and simply employed the Julian calendar with Semitic month names; and a lunar year that is usually, though not always, designated in the documents themselves by the words "in lunar." The latter has never been understood. It is only the ordinary Persian calendar, with the difference that the old Babylonian month names are substituted for the Iranian, the principle being that Nisan, originally the first month, stands for Ferverdin, and so on in regular order: (The corresponding months of the Julian calendar are put in brackets to spare the reader the trouble of referring to the handbooks) Nisan (April), Iyar (May), Khaziran (June), Thamuz (July), Ab (August), Elul (September), First-Teshri (October), Second-Teshri (November), First-Kanun (De-

---

for granted that in 223 the epagomenae preceded Shehriver — quite correctly too, because, even if the shift behind Aban came in the reign of Chosroes I (531-79) and in the earliest possible year, 532, the epagomenae would have preceded Shehriver until 292.

[64] This proves that the reign of Bahram I must be reckoned from September 19, 272 and Nöldeke's chronology (p. 415) slightly corrected. Nöldeke bases his dates, wherever possible, on synchronisms and the coinage, and only as a last resort does he rely exclusively on the various kings' lists (cf. esp. p. 403). The above date supplies precisely the type of synchronism whose absence for this period he regretted (pp. 414. 415 and n. 2). It is, of course, here taken for granted that the reliability of the above documents is superior to that of the Coptic—a fact generally admitted. The question is not gone into in this dissertation because the purpose of the present discussion is to investigate the Persian calendar, not the history of Mani.

[65] Nöldeke, pp. 407 f. 420-22. 424 f.; Michael Kmosko, *S. Simeon bar Sabbae praefatus est . . . (Patrologia Syriaca)* II 690-713. The latter deals specifically only with the date of the persecution of Sapor II.

[66] Nöldeke, pp. 407 f.

cember), Second-Kanun (January), Shebath (February), Adar (March). Some instances of this use of the Persian calendar are the following.

In the Acts of the Martyrs of Karkha.[67] In the eighth year of Yezdegerd II (August 9, 438-57),[68] one group of these martyrs was slain on Friday, Ab 24, a second on Saturday, Ab 25,[69] while the isolated execution of Tohmyazgerd took place on Monday, Elul 25.[70] The dating cannot be that of the Syrian Julian calendar, because, though August 24, 445 fell on a Friday, September 25 came that year on Tuesday, not Monday. According to the Persian reckoning, however, Ab 24 = Murdad 24 = December 28, 445, a Friday;[71] and Elul 25 = Shehriver 25 = January 28, 446, a Monday.[72]

In the Acts of Jacobus Intercisus.[73] He was put to death in 762 Sel., the first year of Bâhram V (August 13, 420-38),[74] on Friday, Second-Teshri 27. 762 Sel. = October 1, 450-51. Second-Teshri 27 = Aban 27 = March 30, 451, a Friday.[75] That the regnal year is wrong happens frequently in these acts;[76] and there is nothing inherently improbable in the years 450-51, the thirteenth year of Yezdegerd II, who persecuted the Church.

In the Acts of Mihrshapur.[77] His martyrdom occurred on Satur-

---

[67] Hoffmann, pp. 43-60; Oskar Braun, *Ausgewählte Akten persischer Märtyrer* (Kempten and Munich 1915), (*Bibliothek der Kirchenväter*), pp. 179-87 (not complete).

[68] Hoffmann, p. 50; Braun, p. 179; cf. Nöldeke, p. 424.

[69] Hoffmann, p. 55; Braun, p. 184; Nöldeke, p. 424.

[70] Hoffmann, p. 58; Braun, p. 187; Nöldeke, p. 424.

[71] Yezdegerd's eighth year began in 445, August 7 = 218. Murdad 24 (epagomenae after Aban) = 4 × 30 + 23 = 143 + 218 = 361 = December 28, 445.

[72] Shehriver 25 = 5 × 30 + 24 = 174 + 218 — 365 = 27 = January 28, 446.

[73] Braun, pp. 150-62; cf. Nöldeke, pp. 420-22.

[74] The correct text is given by Nöldeke, p. 420 and n. 1 (First-Teshri is only a misprint for Second-Teshri, as is shown by the "November" in brackets); Braun, p. 162, adopts the emendation.

[75] New Year's of 450, August 6 = 217. Aban 27 = 7 × 30 + 26 = 236 + 217 — 365 = 88 = March 30, 451.

[76] Cf. Kmosko, II 704.

[77] Nöldeke, p. 421, has everything essential.

day, First-Teshri 10, the second year of Bahram V (August 13, 420-38). The second year of Bahram V began on August 13, 421. First-Teshri 10 = Mehr 10 = February 18, 422, a Saturday.[78] Let these instances suffice to establish the conclusion arrived at earlier in the discussion, namely, that in 590, five days were suppressed and that the civil year had as a consequence begun proportionately later in 589. The further inference is justified that in 408 the epagomenae were transferred to the end of Aban. It does not depend on Albiruni's authority alone, but follows also from the date of the Syriac acts of the martyrs. These dates, falling as they do after the reign of Yezdegerd I, work out exactly on the basis that Second-Teshri preceded the epagomenae. The Manichaean documents give information on the earlier period. Presupposing a New Year's Day of September 19 for 272, they show that the epagomenae were not omitted between that date and 590. The position of the epagomenae at the end of Murdad has a very special interest. Since a cycle of 120 years finished in 280-88, and since the previous intercalation must therefore have been made around 168 A. D., the religious calendar existed before ever the Sassanid dynasty came to the throne, and it had been bequeathed them by their Parthian predecessors.[79]

To give a detailed account of the civil year before 273 would carry this dissertation beyond its scope, but the following may be noticed. Nöldeke, citing a passage from the Fihrist that Sapor I (241-72) [80] took the crown on Sunday, Nisan 1, when the sun stood in the Ram, first establishes the impossibility of interpreting the date in terms of the Julian calendar, and finally arrives at March 20, 242 as a likely equivalent.[81] Now, the Syriac practise of using

---

[78] August 13 = 224. Mehr 10 = 6 × 30 + 9 = 189. 189 + 224 — 365 = 48 = February 18.

[79] Albiruni (Ginzel, I 292) makes some remarks about the neglect of the adjustment and Ginzel, p. 297, assumes that he is referring to Sassanid times. But since the month was intercalated with scrupulous exactness and regularity from 168 to 408, and since the context mentions the destruction of order in the realm, the Arabic author is rather thinking of the insertion of sixty days made by the Abbasid caliph al-Mutadid in 825-26 A.D.; cf. J. Markwart, " Das *Nauroz*, seine Geschichte und seine Bedeutung," *Modi Mem. Vol.*, p. 714.

[80] P. 412, n. 2.   [81] *Ibid.*, 412 f.

Semitic names for the months and the common Persian habit of
referring to the fixed year by the signs of the zodiac,[82] point to the
conclusion that Nisan 1 simply means Ferverdin 1 of the religious
calendar, i e., the *Nauruz*. This presents a difficulty. In 242 the
epagomenae followed Murdad; therefore, Ferverdin 1 = Shehriver
1 = March 1, 242, a Tuesday, not Sunday.[83] While, on the other
hand, the *Great Nauruz*, Ferverdin 6 = Shehriver 6 = March 6,
242 did fall on Sunday, and it is not absurd to imagine that Nisan
1 was used as a rough translation of the New Year's Day *par excel-
lence,* nevertheless, such an interpretation would scarcely be in
keeping with the normal usage of the Syriac-speaking population.
What, then, must be concluded? Did the coronation of Sapor I
occur in a year when the *Nauruz* fell on a Sunday? It would have
happened in 240 and involves further revision of the chronology of
the early Sassanid monarchs. Is it rather to be presumed that five
days were again lost in the period previous to 273? This brings
the *Nauruz* down from March 1 to March 6 in 242. To give a
satisfactory answer to either question would mean a search through
the sources for all synchronisms with the Persian calendar and a
thorough study of the material available on the reign of Sapor I,
and any such investigation would far exceed the limits of this work.

On the other hand, for the time after 273 a basis is provided
for calculating any date of the Persian year, religious or civil.
From 168 to 288 the epagomenae are reckoned after Murdad; from
288 to 408, after Shehriver; from 408 onwards, after Aban. The
New Year can be found in the *Revised Table of the Persian New
Year's Day* appended to this study.[84] To find the date of any
feast, take the religious calendar, equate Ferverdin 1 with the
month preceded by the epagomenae, and figure the same day of the
corresponding month in the civil calendar. For example, to find
the date of the feast of *Sedeh* in 591. After 408, the epagomenae
precede Azur; therefore, Azur 1 = Ferverdin 1 of the religious
calendar. The feast of *Sedeh* comes on Behmen 10 of the religious

---

[82] Fird. VI 448. 492, e. g.

[83] New Year of 241, September 27 = 269. Shehriver 1 = 5 × 30 + 5 =
155 + 269 — 365 = 59 = March 1, 242.

[84] *Infra*, p. 22.

calendar, the tenth day of the eleventh month.[85] The eleventh
month from Azur is Mehr, and so *Sedeh* was celebrated on Mehr
10, 591. The civil year of 590 began June 27 and Mehr 10 =
January 2, 591.

The ultimate purpose (to return at length to the issue) of the
whole discussion of the Persian calendar has been to place upon a
sure foundation the assertion that March 9, not July or September,
is the time at which Bahram VI was crowned. This date is established. Not only does it rest upon the exact agreement of Theophylactus Simocatta and Firdausi—an agreement in itself extremely striking to find in a Byzantine historian and a Persian epic
poet, each the typical and conscientious representative of a tradition entirely independent, nay wholly alien—; but it has also stood
the test of proofs so many and varied as to make it a firm basis
upon which to fix the chronology of the Persian Wars of the
Emperor Maurice.

[85] For the religious calendar, *vide* Ginzel, I 289 f.; Christensen, *L'Iran*,
pp. 168-72.

3

REVISED TABLE OF PERSIAN NEW YEAR'S DAY (224-652)

PNY, Persian New Year's Day. EP, epagomenae precede Sh(ehriver) M(ehr), Az(ur). Each date holds for the three following years.

A.D.	PNY	EP	A.D.	PNY	EP	A.D.	PNY	EP
*224	Oct	1 Sh	372	Aug.	25 M	520	July	19 Az
*228	Sept.	30 Sh	376	—	24 M	524	—	18 Az
*232	—	29 Sh	380	—	23 M	528	—	17 Az
*236	—	28 Sh	384	—	22 M	532	—	16 Az
*240	—	27 Sh	388	—	21 M	536	—	15 Az
*244	—	26 Sh	392	—	20 M	540	—	14 Az
*248	—	25 Sh	396	—	19 M	544	—	13 Az
*252	—	24 Sh	400	—	18 M	548	—	12 Az
*256	—	23 Sh	404	—	17 M	‡552	—	11 (6) Az
*260	—	22 Sh	408	—	16 Az	‡556	—	10 (5) Az
*264	—	21 Sh	412	—	15 Az	‡560	—	9 (4) Az
*268	—	20 Sh	416	—	14 Az	‡564	—	8 (3) Az
272	—	19 Sh	420	—	13 Az	‡568	—	7 (2) Az
276	—	18 Sh	424	—	12 Az	‡572	—	6 (1) Az
†280	—	17 ShM	428	—	11 Az	‡576	—	5 (June 30) Az
†284	—	16 ShM	432	—	10 Az	‡580	—	4 (29) Az
288	—	15 M	436	—	9 Az	‡584	—	3 (28) Az
292	—	14 M	440	—	8 Az	‡588	—	2 (27) Az
296	—	13 M	444	—	7 Az	590	June	27 Az
300	—	12 M	448	—	6 Az	592	—	26 Az
304	—	11 M	452	—	5 Az	596	—	25 Az
308	—	10 M	456	—	4 Az	600	—	24 Az
312	—	9 M	460	—	3 Az	604	—	23 Az
316	—	8 M	464	—	2 Az	608	—	22 Az
320	—	7 M	468	—	1 Az	612	—	21 Az
324	—	6 M	472	July	31 Az	616	—	20 Az
328	—	5 M	476	—	30 Az	620	—	19 Az
332	—	4 M	480	—	29 Az	624	—	18 Az
336	—	3 M	484	—	28 Az	628	—	17 Az
340	—	2 M	488	—	27 Az	§632	—	16 Az
344	—	1 M	492	—	26 Az	636	—	15 Az
348	Aug.	31 M	496	—	25 Az	640	—	14 Az
352	—	30 M	500	—	24 Az	644	—	13 Az
356	—	29 M	504	—	23 Az	648	—	12 Az
360	—	28 M	508	—	22 Az	652	—	11 Az
364	—	27 M	512	—	21 Az			
368	—	26 M	516	—	20 Az			

* PNY possibly five days later; *supra*, p. 20.
† Shift of epagomenae cannot be definitely determined; *supra*, p. 14.

‡ Nöldeke's PNY in parentheses.
§ Era of Yezdegerd begins at this date.

PERSIAN CALENDAR

The column " Religious Year " is that by which the religious feasts were fixed. The reader can readily readjust it for the shift of the epagomenae by equating its Ferverdin 1 with the first of the month in the "Normal Civil Year " preceded by them. Note that the Persians did not number their days; each had an individual name throughout the month; numbers have been substituted here for convenience. The " Normal Civil Year " which shows the ordinary business calendar is also the Armenian calendar for this year. The omission of the epagomenae in 590 resulted in the unusual calendar under " Actual Civil Year." For all necessary supplementary information, see Ginzel, *Handbuch der mathematischen und technischen Chronologie* (Leipzig 1906-14), I 275-309.

Normal Civil Year	Religious Year	Actual Civil Year	Julian Calendar
1 Ferverdin	1 Murdad		July 2, 589
1 Urdi Behesht	1 Shehriver		Aug. 1, —
1 Khurdad	1 Mehr		Aug. 31, —
1 Tir	1 Aban		Sept. 30, —
1 Murdad	1 Azur		Oct. 30, —
1 Shehriver	1 Dei		Nov. 29, —
1 Mehr	1 Behmen		Dec. 29, —
1 Aban	1 Esfendarmuz		Jan. 28, 590
10 —	10 —		Febr. 6, —
11 —	11 —		— 7, —
12 —	12 —		— 8, —
13 —	13 —		— 9, —
14 —	14 —		— 10, —
15 Aban	15 Esfendarmuz		Febr. 11, —
16 —	16 —		— 12, —
17 —	17 —		— 13, —
18 —	18 —		— 14, —
19 —	19 —,		— 15, —
30 —	30 —		— 26, —
1 Epagomena	1 Epagomena	1 Azur	Febr. 27, —
2 —	2 —	2 —	— 28, —
3 —	3 —	3 —	Mar. 1, —
4 —	4 —	4 —	— 2, —
5 —	5 —	5 —	— 3, —
1 Azur	1 Ferverdin	6 —	— 4, —
6 —	6 —	11 —	— 9, —
1 Dei	1 Urdi Behesht	6 Dei	Apr. 3, —
1 Behmen	1 Khurdad	6 Behmen	May 3, —
1 Esfendarmuz	1 Tir	6 Esfendarmuz	June 2, —
26 —	26 —	1 FERVERDIN	JUNE 27, 590
1 Ferverdin	1 Murdad	6 —	July 2, 590

CHAPTER II

CHRONOLOGY FROM THE MUTINY OF THE ROMAN ARMY IN SYRIA, APRIL, 21, 588, TO THE CORONATION OF BAHRAM VI, MARCH 9, 590

It has been assumed in the above discussion that Bahram VI was crowned in 590, although, as Azur 11 could coincide with March 9 from 588 to 591, the year still remains to be determined. In favor of 590, there is not only the explicit testimony of the great majority of the sources concerning the accession of Chosroes, but also a diversity of evidence for related events that all converges on that same year.[1]

Accession of Hormisdas IV. Scholars have agreed in fixing the beginning of his reign in February or March 579.[2] The *Chronicon Seert,* however, gives the more exact information that Hormisdas IV was crowned in a fire-temple at Gundeshapur after the death of his father " in the days called *Frordighan* "[3]—an expression that, applying loosely to the whole eleven days of the festival, may here be taken to denote the *Nauruz.* It must be remembered that, according to a contemporary document, the *Letter of Tansar,*[4] the coronation of a Sassanid monarch constituted his official accession and the legal bestowal of his office.[5] Both because Chosroes I, less

---

[1] Theophylactus Simocatta is the basic source.

[2] Franz Dölger, *Regesten der Kaiserurkunden des oströmischen Reiches von 565-1453,* Part I, *Regesten von 565-1025 (Corpus der griech. Urk., A, I,* Munich and Berlin 1924), Nr. 56; Ernst Stein, *Studien zur Geschichte des byzantinischen Reiches* (Stuttgart 1919), pp. 90. 100, n. 3; E. Gerland, " Erich Merten. Zum Perserkriege der byzantinischen Kaiser Justinos II. und Tiberios II.," *Berl. Philol. Wochenschrift,* 33 (1913) 48 f.; J. B. Bury, *A History of the Later Roman Empire from Arcadius to Irene (395 A.D. to 800 A.D.)* (London and New York 1889), II 97. 105; Nöldeke, Tab., pp. 429 f.

[3] *Histoire nestorienne (Chronique de Séert), publiée et traduite par* Addai Scher (Paris 1908-19), *PO* VII 196. الفروزديجان should, of course, be read al-frordighan. [The emendation involves only the removal of the dot from ز. Rev. Dr. Edw. P. Arbez.]

[4] Christensen, *L'Iran,* p. 61, dates it between 557 and 570.

[5] *Ibid.,* p. 259. The *Letter of Tansar* describes how the responsible officers of the realm determine the candidate for the throne in secret deliberation,

than a week before his death, had secured the undisputed succession of his high-born son,[6] and because the Persians, due to the extreme danger of internecine strife that was always at hand, but particularly during an interregnum, would proceed at the earliest possible moment to provide themselves with a legitimate and recognized head, it may be presumed that events followed their normal course and that the new king took possession of his throne on the first day suitable for the ceremony. The epagomenae were ill-omened,[7] but the *Nauruz* was a traditional coronation day.[8] The accession of Hormisdas IV, therefore, occurred on Azur 1, i. e., March 7, 579.[9] It is described by Menander as occurring in winter,[10] by Theophylactus at the beginning of spring;[11] the former with greater scientific exactness, the latter following, with equal justice, the popular Persian usage.

and how the result of their choice becomes public only at the moment, and precisely by the act, of coronation.

[6] Theophyl. Sim. III 16, 7; Tab., Nöld., p. 252; ChrS *PO* VII 196; Fird. VI 436; *The Chronicle of* JOHN, *Bishop of* NIKIU, *Translated from Zotenberg's Ethiopic Text by* R. H. Charles (London and Oxford 1916), Ch. 95, par. 25; *Abu Hanifa ad-*DINAWERI. *Kitab al-akhbar at-tiwal, publié par* V. Guirgass (Leiden 1888), p. 76; *Contextio gemmarum, sive* EUTYCHII *patriarchae Alexandrini annales interprete* E. Pocock, *MPG* 57, 713 C; *Chronique de Abou-Djafar-Mohammed-ben-Djarir-ben-Yezid Tabari, traduite sur la version persane d'Abou-Ali-Mohammed* BELAMI *par* H. Zotenberg (Paris 1867-74), II 246; Edward G. Browne, "Some Account of the Arabic Work Entitled 'NIHAYATU'l-irab fi akhbari'l-Fars wa'l-Arab,' particularly of that Part which Treats of the Persian Kings," *Journal Roy. As. Soc.,* 1900, p. 232; *Histoire des rois de Perse de la dynastie des Sassanides, traduite du persan de* MIRKHOND *par* A. I. Silvestre de Sacy (*Mémoires sur diverses antiquités de la Persé,* Paris 1793), pp. 387 f.; *Histoire des rois des Perses par Abu Mansur Abd al-Malik ibn Mohammed ibn Ismail al-*THAALIBI, *texte arabe publié et traduit par* H. Zotenberg (Paris 1900), p. 637. All these sources mention the fact that Chosroes I appointed his own successor; for the interval between this act and his death, Thaalibi gives a week, but Firdausi a year. The latter seems to be quite improbable: an heir apparent universally acknowledged as such for a year would in the Persian Empire have been a serious rival to the reigning monarch himself.

[7] *Supra*, p. 11.　　　　　　　[8] *Supra*, p. 9.

[9] For all these reductions, see *Persian Calendar, supra*, p. 23. In 579, the *Nauruz* would be three days later than in 590.

[10] *Exc. Const.*, I[1] 213.

[11] III 16, 7; cf. Nöldeke, Tab., pp. 429 f.

Deposition of Hormisdas. For this event, there are only the royal lists to depend on,[12] which give to Hormisdas IV, 11 years, 7 months, 10 days.[13] It has been mentioned above that the practise prevailed among the Persians of making the king's years coincide with the civil calendar.[14] As a result, the numbers for the length of a reign are always open to two interpretations: either they denote the actual time during which the royal power was exercised, or include in the first year the period from the previous New Year's Day to the accession. In the latter case the 7 months, 10 days, state simply the length of Hormisdas' reign in his last year.[15] This must be the meaning of the figures in the present instance, since he was deposed before March 9. As an Arabic calculation ordinarily includes the last day, the deposition of Hormisdas IV took place on Aban 10, i. e., February 6, 590.

Coronation of Chosroes II. According to Tabari, the Hegira (July 16, 622) occurred 32 years, 5 months, 15 days, after the accession of Chosroes II.[16] In 622, the New Year's Day being June 19, July 16 fell on Ferverdin 28. If one reckons back 165 days inclusively, with the epagomenae before Azur, one arrives at Aban 19, and, subtracting 32 years, one gets Aban 19, 590. If, however, the epagomenae, which were suppressed in 590, be disregarded, the result is Aban 14. Now which calculation seems the more likely to have been made by Tabari? Had the Arabs any means of knowing that the Persians suppressed the intercalary period? So far as is discernible, none. Albiruni, who was certainly well informed about the calendar, says nothing of so unprecedented an alteration. If, then, Tabari found Aban 19 in a text, he would have calculated the epagomenae before Azur as a matter of course, and so found his sum of 165 days. From Aban 14, it would have

[12] Nöldeke, *ibid.*, p. 431.
[13] Tab., Nöld., p. 275; *vide* Thaal., p. 661. The text reads 9 months, but cf. Nöldeke, p. 431, n. 1. In al-Maqdisi and ibn Qutaiba, 7 is found. Cf. *Le livre de la création et de l'histoire de Motahhar ben Tahir el-*MAQDISI *attribué à Abou-Zeid Ahmed ben Sahl el-Balkhi publié et traduit . . . par* Cl. Huart (*Publications de l'École des Langues Orientales Vivantes*, Paris 1899-1919), III 172; *Ibn Ooteiba's Handbuch der Geschichte . . . herausgegeben von* F. Wüstenfeld (Göttingen 1850), p. 329.
[14] *Supra*, p. 14.   [15] Nöldeke, Tab., pp. 404 f.
[16] *Ibid.*, pp. 360 f.; Dinawari, p. 76, has a false reckoning.

been for him 170 days to Ferverdin 28. Chosroes. II, therefore, began his reign on Aban 19, February 15, 590.

The same year 590 is given by almost all the other sources. The text of Sebeos [17] is, unfortunately, mutilated at this point, but Thomas Ardzruni,[18] who depends entirely upon him in this portion of his work, adds " In the eighth year of Maurice," i. e., August 14, 589-90.[19] The same date is found in Thomas of Marga,[20] Agapius of Hierapolis,[21] Michael Syrus,[22] Bar-Hebraeus,[23] and John of

[17] *Histoire d'Héraclius par l'Évêque* SEBÊOS, *traduite de l'arménien et annotée par* F. Macler (Paris 1904), p. 11.

[18] THOMAS ARDZROUNI, x^e *siècle, traduit par* M. Brosset (*Collection d'historiens arméniens*, St. Petersburg 1874-76), I 76.

[19] Nöldeke, Tab., pp. 430 f., who entertains a very poor opinion of Armenian sources, attaches no importance to this testimony. If it really goes back to Sebeos, it is, notwithstanding, of great value; only one cannot be too sure that it does, as it is omitted by Stephen of Taron, who depends on Sebeos quite as much as Thomas Ardzruni; cf. *Des* STEPHANOS VON TARON *armenische Geschichte aus dem Altarmenischen übersetzt von* H. Gelzer and A. Burckhardt (*Scriptores sacri et profani*, fasc. iv, Leipzig 1907), p. 81.

[20] *The Book of Governors: the Historia Monastica of* THOMAS, *Bishop of* MARGA, A. D. *840* tr. by E. A. Wallis Budge (London 1893), II 79. He puts the accession of Chosroes in 901 Sel., i. e., October 1, 589-90. This is the same text as that cited by Nöldeke, p. 431, n. 3, from Joseph Simonius Assemanus, *Bibliotheca orientalis Clementino-Vaticana* (Rome 1719-28) III¹ 458b. 471a. The reference to *ibid.*, III¹ 187, from which Nöldeke concludes that Chosroes' first year was 902 Sel., i. e., 590-91, is again precisely the same passage of Thomas of Marga, save that Assemani equates Chosroes' fifth year with 906 Sel. For this there is no justification, in Budge's translation at least, which reads only that Chosroes' first year was 901 Sel., and goes on to speak of an event of his fifth year, but without mention of any corresponding year Sel.

[21] *Kitab al-Unvan. Histoire universelle écrite par* AGAPIUS (*Mahboub*) *de Menbidj, éditée et traduite en français par* A. Vasiliev (Paris 1910-15) *PO* VIII 441.

[22] *Chronique de* MICHEL LE SYRIEN, *patriarche jacobite d'Antioche (1166-1199), éditée pour la première fois et traduite en français par* J.-B. Chabot (Paris 1899-1924) II 360.

[23] *Gregorii* BARHEBRAEI *chronicon ecclesiasticum quod . . . latinitate donarunt* J.-B. Abbeloos et T. J. Lamy (Paris and Louvain 1872-77) III 106; *The Chronography of Gregory Abul Faraj the Son of Aaron, the Hebrew Physician, Commonly Known as* BAR HEBRAEUS . . . , *translated from the Syriac by* E. A. Wallis Budge (London 1932) I 85. This latter

Biclar.[24] The statement of Pseudo-Sebeos [25] and Eutychius [26] that Chosroes came to the throne in Maurice's seventh year, August 14, 588-89, is explained readily enough if they took for granted that he counted his reign in the normal fashion from the New Year's Day previous to his accession.

For the events between the deposition of Hormisdas and the accession of Chosroes, there is but one indication of the chronology; namely, that the young prince received the news when the first night of the new moon had passed.[27] The new moon in February 590 fell on February 10.[28] This notice, surprisingly enough, agrees quite well with the rest of the data.

Interval Between Coronation of Chosroes and Accession of Bahram. For this period, on the other hand, events can be arranged day by day, principally on the basis of Theophylactus, but with the aid also of the other sources. The chronology has a special interest because of the suppression of the epagomenae in 590, and because it offers a confirmation of the date for Chosroes' coronation.[29] After narrating the coronation, the Greek historian tells of the assassination of Hormisdas and adds that negotiations were opened with Bahram on the sixth day; but the sixth day after what, whether after the election of the new king or the murder of the old, he does not specify.[30] The other writers, however, lay particular emphasis on the haste with which Bahram descended on Ctesiphon, and Thaalibi writes that he appeared on the Naharwan, a canal twelve miles east of Ctesiphon, before a week had passed after the elevation of Chosroes.[31] This leaves no doubt as to Theophylactus' mean-

work of Bar-Hebraeus is almost verbatim from Michael Syrus and will not be quoted again unless it adds important information.

[24] Iohannis *abbatis monasterii* Biclarensis *chronica edidit* Th. Mommsen (Berlin 1894), *MGH, auct. antiq.* XI, *Chron. min.* II 219.

[25] Frédéric Macler, " Pseudo-Sebêos, texte arménien traduit et annoté," *Journal Asiatique*[10] 6 (1905) 149.

[26] *MPG* 57, 717 C.   [27] Fird. VII 1.

[28] Dr. A. James Robertson, Director of the U. S. Naval Observatory at Washington, D. C., was kind enough to supply this information.

[29] Cf. *supra*, pp. 10 f.   [30] IV 7, 5.

[31] Seb., p. 14; Din., p. 89; Tab. Nöld., pp. 273. 277; Maqd. III 172; Bel. II 275 f.; Fird. VII 6 f.; Nih., p. 238; ChrS *PO* XIII 444; *The Ecclesiastical History of* Evagrius *with the Scholia* ed. by J. Bidez and L. Parmentier

ing; namely, that negotiations were opened with Bahram (Item 1)[32] five days after the coronation. Chosroes receives the answer and one day later (Item 2) calls a council.[33] He then leads his own troops forth from the capital and engages his antagonist in a long parley.[34] This makes one more day (Item 3). Theophylactus hints this clearly enough, because messages go to and fro from dawn until dusk,[35] and Firdausi explicitly states that, the night having passed in camp, the conversations began early on the next morning.[36] It presents something of a puzzle, however, to determine how long the two armies faced each other before the decisive battle. While the other sources give attention only to the principal occurrences,[37] Theophylactus relates that Chosroes began preparations for the flight on the second day,[38] and that Bahram attacked on the night of the seventh day.[39] He does not, however, make clear whether the latter is inclusive or exclusive of the former; if exclusive, the final encounter was on the ninth day (Item 4) after the parley; if inclusive, on the seventh (Item 4). In any event, it was on the following day (Item 5) that Chosroes fled, and that Bahram sent his cavalry in hot pursuit. He would, of course, lose no time in attempting to capture the fugitive.[40] The king escaped, but his maternal uncle, Bindoes, was brought back a prisoner on the seventh day (Item 6).[41]

The interval from the coronation of Chosroes, February 15, to the accession of Bahram, March 9, consists of 22 days. If the *items* given above are added, the sum amounts to 22 or 20 days; the latter being the more probable, and for the following reason. All the sources that give in detail Bahram's history as tyrant do so on the occasion of Bindoes' return to Ctesiphon and presuppose

---

(London 1898), (*Byzantine Texts edited by J. B. Bury*), VI 17; *Ibn-Wadhih qui dicitur al-*JAQUBI *historiae*, ed. by M. Th. Houtsma (Leiden 1883) I 191; MAÇOUDI. *Les prairies d'or, texte et traduction par* C. Barbier de Meynard and Pavet de Courteille (Paris 1861-77) II 215; *Chronicon anonymum interpretatus est* I. Guidi, *OSCO, scr. Syri*, III, 4, *Chr. min.* (Paris and Leipzig 1903), p. 15.

[32] The indications of time are itemized, *Item 1, 2,* etc., for convenience of reference.

[33] IV 8, 1.   [34] IV 9, 1-4.   [35] IV 9, 4.   [36] VII 10.

[37] Cf. *supra*, p. 28, n. 31. *Vide*, in addition, Fird. VII 36-42.

[38] IV 9, 8.   [39] IV 9, 9.   [40] IV 12, 1.   [41] IV 12, 2.

that it preceded the actual usurpation of the throne.[42] Firdausi, however, gives the most minute account: Bahram called a council of the nobility on the day after Bindoes fell into his hands [43] and on the following morning took the crown.[44] The accuracy of this version is confirmed by everything that is known of the circumstances. The usurper desired supremely to give an air of legitimacy to his position [45] and would have undoubtedly waited for news of the death of the rightful monarch before taking any positive steps. Instead, it became known to all that Chosroes had escaped but had suffered the humiliation of accepting protection from the very rival with respect to whom the Persians had ever been most sensitive about their national honor. Bahram could well have felt that the splendor of his own achievements as the conqueror of the Asiatic nomad, Iran's secular enemy, rendered him, by contrast with the pitiful condition of a king who was prisoner in all but name, the logical candidate for the throne. His triumph won him the spontaneous support of the army; it might gain also for him, if only the opportunity were properly presented, the enthusiastic acclamation of the nobles. He failed. The assembly broke up in tumult,[46] and he dared risk no delay. There is no good reason, therefore, to reject Firdausi's two-day interval for the council and the coronation. This gives the following chronology: Chosroes II is crowned, February 15; negotiates with Bahram, February 20; calls council and marches to Naharwan, February 21; holds parley with the rebel, February 22; loses the night battle, February 28; flees and is pursued, March 1; Bindoes is brought back, March 7; Bahram calls together the nobles, March 8; takes the crown, March 9. The intercalary days should have been from February 27 to March 3. Even if Bahram seized the throne on the very day that Bindoes was brought back, the decisive battle would still have to be dated on March 2 and the flight of Chosroes on March 3, both within the ill-omened epagomenae.[47]

A final proof of the above chronology is to be found in a document from Chosroes' own hand, which, recorded by both Theo-

---

[42] Tab. Nöld., p. 282; Din., p. 94; Bel. II 284 f.

[43] VII 56.

[44] VII 62 f.

[45] Theophyl. Sim. IV 12, 3-5.

[46] Fird. VII 61.

[47] Cf. *supra*, pp. 10 f.

phylactus [48] and Evagrius,[49] testifies that January 7, and February 9, 591 were still within his first year.[50] This statement, though it raises a very difficult question,[51] agrees with the conclusions reached above.

Early in 590, then, is the time, by almost unanimous agreement of the sources, of the coronation of Chosroes II. The chronology of events from 588 to 590 may now be studied.

Mutiny of the Roman Army. In 588, the Roman troops in Syria broke out in revolt.[52] The year is given by Evagrius. He relates that a new general, Priscus, was appointed on the eastern front to succeed Philippicus and to carry out a decree reducing the pay [53] and that, in their resentment, the soldiers repudiated both him and the Emperor.[54] The revolt, the historian goes on, continued into the following winter, during which the city of Antioch was leveled by an earthquake.[55] The disaster occurred in October 637, Era of Antioch.[56] As this era started on September 1, 49 B. C.,[57] the year of the mutiny was 588. Though Evagrius does not say in so many words that the uprising began in the same year that the city was destroyed, still the whole tenor of his narrative supposes it. Any doubt is removed by Michael Syrus. He states that the army expelled the general in the sixth year of Maurice, August 14, 587-88, and explicitly vouches for the fact that the shock came in the ensuing winter.[58] Agapius, properly understood, also supports this view.[59]

---

[48] V 13, 4-6.   [49] VI 21.

[50] Theophyl. Sim. V 13, 5 f.; Evagr., *loc. cit.*

[51] Cf. *infra*, pp. 51 f.

[52] Theophyl. Sim. III 1, 9–III 5, 10; Evagr. VI 4-6. 9-13; Agap. Hier. *PO* VIII 440 f.; Mich. Syr. II 359.

[53] VI 4; cf. Theophyl. Sim. III 1, 2. 9.

[54] VI 5; Theophyl. Sim. III 2, 8.

[55] VI 8; cf. Mich. Syr., *loc. cit.*

[56] The earthquake occurred probably on October 29; cf. Agap. Hier. *PO* VIII 440. Evagrius' phrase κατὰ τὴν ἔνην καὶ νέαν ἡμέραν, which applied strictly to the thirtieth day of the classical lunar month and then was extended to the last day of any month even if it had only 29 days, is most likely to be understood here of October 29, not October 31.

[57] Ginzel, *Handb. d. Chron.* III 43 f.; cf. *infra*, pp. 40 f.

[58] *Loc. cit.*

[59] Agapius uses the same source as Michael Syrus, but by taking the

More Detailed Chronology of the Mutiny. Priscus joined the men in their camp at Monocarton just before Easter, April 18, 588.[60] Nothing happened on the feast itself nor on the two following days, but the storm broke on Wednesday, April 21.[61] Maurice finally removed Priscus and reinstated Philippicus, but too late. The army had already made up its mind no longer to recognize the Emperor. The movement had crystallized into determined opposition both to him and the former leader, all this having taken shape four months before the devastation of Antioch, i. e., by the end of June 588.[62] In the meantime, Hormisdas made one puny effort to attack Roman territory.[63] This attack, paradoxical as it may seem, served to divert the attention of the rebels, who allowed themselves to be persuaded by Germanus, a leader of their own choice, to repulse it, and then to make two successive invasions of enemy territory. The second invasion ended in a signal victory. They turned suddenly at Martyropolis on the Persians who were pursuing them and slew the opposing general, Maruzas.[64] The course of Theophylactus' narrative would induce the reader to place this triumph comparatively late in the year, since at this point the advent of winter is noted.[65]

Battle in Bznunis. Sebeos mentions that Aphraates won a battle at Calkadzhur in the canton of Bznunis, at the west end of Lake Van. He places it after the return of the marzban from a defeat, which was ultimately converted into a victory, at Nisibis.[66] There is considerable confusion in all this; for, at Nisibis, Aphraates was left dead on the field.[67] Since he had succeeded to the command of Nisibis in 589 he certainly never went back to Armenia after that date.[68] He had, however, held office in Armenia for four years

---

earthquake item out of its proper context, he gets it in the wrong year of Maurice. Such questions will be fully discussed in Part II of the present work.

[60] Theophyl. Sim. III 1, 4.
[61] *Id.*, III 1, 9.   [62] Evagr. VI 8; cf. end of VI 7.
[63] Theophyl. Sim. III, 3, 8; cf. Evagr. VI 9; Mich. Syr., *loc. cit.*
[64] Theophyl. Sim. III 3, 10–III 4, 4; III 5, 8.
[65] III 4, 6.
[66] P. 10; no other source records it. Cf. *infra*, p. 34, n. 80.
[67] Theophyl. Sim. III 6, 3.   [68] *Ibid.*; cf. *infra*, p. 34.

previously, as Stein shows.[69] A difficulty, however, arises from the fact that before 589 the Romans carried on no offensive there whatever.[70] The question naturally occurs as to whom Aphraates did defeat at Calkadzhur. The answer suggests itself that it was the mutinous army from Mesopotamia. Presumably, Aphraates anticipated just such irregularities, met the troops at the border and turned them back, perhaps by a mere threat, without actually coming to grips. Whether the incident took place on the first or the second invasion of the rebels, is, of course, impossible to say. It seems likely, at any rate, that the battle of Bznunis was fought in 588.

End of Mutiny. The army, though considerably mollified by this time, still refused to acknowledge Philippicus as its general. The condition lasted throughout 588 and well into 589.[71] Finally the soldiers yielded the point and Gregory, Patriarch of Antioch, won them back to their leader. This happened in Holy Week, either on Monday, April 4, 589, which Evagrius seems to say,[72] or on Holy Thursday, April 7, 589, as Nicephorus Callistus Xanthopulus understands Evagrius' phrase.[73]

Fall of Martyropolis. Immediately afterwards, the Roman cause suffered a severe setback, the loss of Martyropolis.[74] No source mentions the exact date, though both Theophylactus and Evagrius emphasize its proximity to the reconciliation on April 4 or 7, 589, and give valuable chronological indications. Directly upon the successful termination of his plea to the mutineers, Gregory sent word to Maurice and also to Philippicus, who had meantime reached Tarsus on his way to Constantinople.[75] Maurice then ordered the general to return to Antioch.[76] This exchange of letters took no

[69] *Stud. z. Gesch. d. byz. Reiches*, p. 50, n. 2.
[70] The discussion of this question is reserved for Part III of the present work.
[71] Theophyl. Sim. III 5, 9; Evagr. VI 13.
[72] *Ibid.*; cf. Henricus Valesius, *Evagrii scholastici Epiphaniensis et ex praefectis ecclesiasticae historiae libri sex, H. V. interprete, MPG* 86², 2863 D.
[73] *Ecclesiastica historia, MPG* 147, 360 D.
[74] Theophyl. Sim. III 5, 11; Evagr. VI 14; Agap. Hier. *PO* VIII 440; Mich. Syr. II 360.
[75] Evagr. VI 13.   [76] Theophyl. Sim. III 5, 10.

more than a month and may have required much less time.[77] Allowing for the news of the disaster to reach Syria from Armenia IV, one may with certainty place the fall of Martyropolis before the middle of May 589.

Battle of Martyropolis. Philippicus hastened with the army to Martyropolis. After his attempts to take the city by storm proved futile, he desisted, confining his efforts to preventing the reinforcement of the small Persian garrison.[78] Hormisdas determined at all costs to hold the fortress. Knowing that Mebodes, the marzban of Nisibis, did not have sufficient men to relieve the beleaguered town, he ordered Aphraates, marzban of Armenia, to help him with the soldiers under his command.[79] In a great battle, the Persians were worsted. Mebodes lost his life, but Aphraates succeeded, in spite of this, in throwing enough strength into the hard pressed citadel to save it.[80] Though Evagrius, through some confusion, puts this battle in a later year than he should, his statement may be accepted that it occurred in summer, probably not much later than July 1, 589.[81] This estimate is based on the hypothesis that, if Martyropolis fell before the middle of May, Aphraates would have almost immediately been ordered thither and, as the garrison was in dire straits, he would have lost no time in forcing a decision.

Chronology of the Marzbans of Armenia. In Sebeos' list of the Persian marzbans of Armenia [82] Stein has solved the major chronological difficulties.[83] But, in his dates for the " great aspet " (579-86), Aphraates (586-90), and Hrartin Datan (590-92), some trifling corrections must be made. As just shown, Aphraates was ordered to Martyropolis about May 589. At the battle of Solachon

---

[77] A. M. Ramsay, "The Speed of the Roman Imperial Post," *Journal of Roman Studies*, 15 (1925) 63. 73. The distance from Constantinople to Antioch was 750 miles (Roman), the ordinary rate of the courier fifty miles a day.

[78] Evagr. VI 14; Theophyl. Sim. III 5, 14; Agap. Hier. *PO* VIII 441; Mich. Syr., *loc. cit.*

[79] Theophyl. Sim. III 5, 14 f.; Seb., p. 10, and cf. *supra*, p. 32.

[80] Theophyl. Sim. III 5, 15; Evagr. VI 14; Seb., p. 10, may be thinking of this battle (cf. *supra*, p. 32, n. 66).

[81] *Loc. cit.*   [82] Pp. 9-11.

[83] *Stud. z. Gesch. d. byz. Reiches*, p. 50, n. 2.

early in 585,[84] Aphraates had distinguished himself.[85] It is likely that, as a reward for his services, he was shortly afterwards promoted to marzban of Armenia. His term ran, then, from the latter half of 585 to May 589, not 586 to 590. The " great aspet " must have been superseded in 585, not 586. According to Sebeos, Hrartin Datan succeeded to Aphraates and held office for two years. This can hardly be right because Bahram removed Hormisdas' appointees in March 590 when he usurped the throne.[86]

It has been shown,[87] with respect to the Romans, that Maurice had his hands full with the mutiny from April 21, 588 to April 7, 589, and that, no sooner had he solved the one difficulty than the fall of Martyropolis confronted him with another. On the Persian side, Hormisdas, who had scarcely availed himself at all of the magnificent opportunity presented in 588 by the anarchy among his enemies, found himself early in 589 in a position to dispatch his army out of Armenia to consolidate his chance gains on the Syrian front. This fact may be explained by determining the simultaneous chronology of Persian affairs.

The Turkish Invasion of Persia. This momentous event having set in motion the train of causes that ultimately brought about the downfall of Hormisdas receives due attention from all sources for the history of the Sassanids. Many of these closely associate it with other hostile movements—an Arab incursion into lower Mesopotamia, a " Chazar " raid on Azerbaijan, a gigantic Roman offensive against Nisibis.[88] Four of the sources date the Turkish invasion in the eleventh year of Hormisdas, July 2, 588-89.[89] The

---

[84] For the date, *vide infra*, pp. 55 ff.

[85] Theophyl. Sim. II 4, 4 f.; cf. II 3, 1-3.

[86] Bel. II 285 f.   [87] *Supra*, pp. 31-33.

[88] Theophyl. Sim. III 6, 9-15; Evagr. VI 15; Seb., pp. 11 f.; M. Brosset, *Histoire de la Géorgie depuis l'antiquité jusqu'au xixᵉ siècle traduite du géorgien* (St. Petersburg 1849-51), I¹ 221; Qut., p. 328;Yaq. I 187 f.; Din., pp. 81 f.; Tab., Nöld., pp. 269 f.; Eut. *MPG* 57, 716 B; Maqd. III 172; Mas. II 211 f.; Bel. II 248-50. 251 f.; Thaal., pp. 642 f.; Fird. VI 456-60; Mirkh., pp. 389-91; ChrS *PO* XIII 443; Nih., p. 233; Agap. Hier. *PO* VIII 441; Anon. Guidi, p. 15.

[89] Din., p. 81; Tab., Nöld., p. 269; Mas. II 211; Fird. VI 456.

only author that imparts more precise information is Firdausi. According to him, the first great battle was fought against the Turks "when the sun rose in the sign of the Lion," i. e., July 22-August 21, 588,[90] and the whole campaign was over by April 8, 589.[91] It would be most surprising to find these notices inaccurate. The Persian general was Bahram, and the renown of his exploit lived on in song and legend. Many a rapt listener was stirred with the story of that day when he returned from Balkh, the capital of barbaric kings. That was an unforgettable day, on which the hero, fresh from the glorious victory that delivered his native land from the secular enemy, came home at the head of an exultant army to Rai, the city that had given him birth. Very likely, it became an annual holiday. It was the "happy" day Khurdad of the month Dei, the sixth day of the tenth month, April 8, 589.

Bahram's Invasion of Suania. Upon the completion of the campaign against the Turks, Bahram was ordered to make a descent upon the Roman dependency in the Caucasus, Suania. Theophylactus alone mentions this expedition. He dates it in the eighth year of Maurice, August 14, 589-90.[92] This requires more precise definition, particularly as it seems on first thought not to agree well with the date given by Firdausi for Bahram's return. The discrepancy is, however, only apparent and disappears entirely on closer study. Immediately after the invasion of Suania, Bahram came down out of Azerbaijan and took up a position on the Greater Zab.[93] In order to reach that vantage point he must have crossed the mountains between Lake Urmia and the Tigris basin by the Keli-Shin Pass. This is usually closed by snow about the end of October.[94] November 1 is, then, the *terminus ad quem* for

---

[90] VI 492.   [91] VI 554.   [92] III 6, 7.   [93] IV 1, 6.

[94] H. C. Rawlinson, "Notes on a Journey to Tabriz, through Persian Kurdistan, to the Ruins of Takhti-Soleiman . . . ," *Journal R. Geogr. Soc.*, 10 (1841) 20 f.: "The only times at which the mountain can be ascended in safety are the first fortnight in October and the last in March. . . . I have already alluded to the danger of traversing this pass—it arises not so much from the depth of the snow (for an active mountaineer, by threading his way along the most exposed points, can generally avoid this difficulty), as from the violent and deadly drifts which keep continually sweeping over the face of the mountains during the greater part of the winter months. These drifts come on so suddenly, and with such terrific fury, that a travel-

the events of 589 down to Bahram's arrival at the Zab. Bahram had first to proceed from Rai to Suania. Theophylactus narrates that he took the route up the Araxes[95] (presumably over the pass through Akhalkalaki and Akhalzikh)[96] into Suania and then retired all the way down the Araxes into distant Albania, from one end of the Caucasus to the other.[97] It was from this place that he marched to the Zab. By rough measurement it is 800 miles from Rai to Suania, 500 back to the approximate site of the battle in Albania, and 450 from that point to Mosul.[98] It is impossible to

ler who is once fairly caught in them will rarely escape, and as at the same time the pass of Keli-Shin is the only line of communication between Persia and Rowandiz, and parties are thus found at all seasons who are bold enough to attempt to traverse it, a winter is never known to elapse without several persons being here lost in the snow."

[95] III 6, 16.

[96] The geographical data depend upon the maps in *Stieler's Atlas of Modern Geography* (10th ed., completely revised and largely redrawn under the direction of Professor Dr. H. Haack, Gotha 1930-31), I, Nrs. 65 and 59. The reader may with equal convenience consult the maps accompanying the following works: W. E. D. Allen, *A History of the Georgian People* (London 1932); H. Hübschmann, "Die altarmenischen Ortsnamen mit Beiträgen zur historischen Topographie Armeniens und einer Karte," *Indogermanische Forschungen* 16 (1904) 197-490; H. F. B. Lynch, *Armenia. Travels and Studies* (London, New York, Bombay 1901); Ernst Honigmann, *Die Ostgrenze des byzantinischen Reiches von 363 bis 1071. . . .* (A. A. Vasiliev, *Byzance et les Arabes, Vol. III*, i. e., *Corpus Bruxellense Historiae Byzantinae, No. 3*, Brussels 1935). Honigmann and Hübschmann do not mark the highways: ancient Rai stands close to modern Teheran and a road runs almost straight to Tabriz. It enters Armenia just where the Araxes turns northeast to run into the Kur (or the Caspian), follows the Araxes roughly to the Arpa-chaï, takes this tributary through ancient Ani to the east of Lake Chaldyr, thence north to Akhalkalaki, etc.

[97] III 6, 17.

[98] These measurements have been made on Haack-Stieler's maps, and will do for present purposes. The following information offers a basis of comparison. Lynch traveled over the very pass supposedly used by Bahram, and gives a very fine description of the whole route through Akhalzikh to Alexandropol (now Leninakan), *op. cit.*, I 48-123. Measured on the map, it is 128 miles from Kutais to Leninakan. In Lynch, it is 158 miles from Kutais to Jellap and then about 100 minutes' more riding into Leninakan—altogether not less than 170 miles. This is a representative section of the way. The actual distance traveled by Lynch averages nearly a third greater than that found by measurements on the map.

4

crowd a march of 1750 miles together with all the other events narrated by Theophylactus [89] into the seventy days between August 14 and November 1. Obviously, the date, the eighth year of Maurice, applies only to the crucial moments of the campaign, the battle and its significant aftermath. Firdausi's *terminus a quo,* April 8, is itself none too early.

Invasion of the " Chazars." Allusion is made above to the statements of various sources that Persia faced a fourfold invasion in 588-89.[100]   One of these incursions in particular will now be noticed; namely, that of the " Chazars." [101]   With regard to this the *Georgian Chronicle* furnishes the independent and important evidence that follows.   Guaram Curopalates, having received for the purpose a very considerable sum of money from Maurice, induced the wild tribes of the Caucasus and the north to pour down into Azerbaijan.   Startled in the midst of their plundering by the sudden news of Bahram's return, the invaders hurriedly withdrew. Guaram, fearing reprisals, fortified his country; he was, however, relieved of all further anxiety by the revolt of Bahram.[102]   The remark about Bahram's return is extremely significant: it shows, since the Persian general reached Rai April 8, 589, that the raid had been planned for that year and that it must have gotten off only to a fair start when it had to stop.   It may, of course, be taken for granted—for the *Georgian Chronicle* knows nothing of the invasion of Suania—that it was really the approach of the Persian army, not the mere threat of it, that scared off the freebooters. The raid of the " Chazars," therefore, lasted for a short while after April 589.

Revolt in Armenia. Theophylactus dates this revolt in 589.[103] He stops his narrative of the invasion of Suania at the moment that Bahram repudiated Hormisdas. He then introduces the Armenian incident and says that it had happened a short time before.   By this rather vague reference he may mean either a short time before Bahram openly revolted or a short time before the whole sequence

[89] III 6, 16–III 8, 3; III 8, 10 f.   [100] *Supra,* p. 35 and n. 88.

[101] Yaq., Din., Tab., Maqd., Mas., Bel., Fird., Nih., *loc. cit.*

[102] *Hist. de la Géorgie,* I[1] 221. This work is also known as the *Georgian Chronicle.*

[103] III 8, 4-8.

of events which culminated in his revolt; but, in any case, he sets
the uprising in 589. Sebeos, however, puts it after the peace between Chosroes II and Maurice, that is, after 591.[104] There cannot be the slightest question that the Greek historian is immeasur-
ably the better authority. In this very instance, his sober account
presents a striking contrast to the fantastic legend woven into the
Armenian's story. If the choice were made on grounds of general
reliability, then, it could simply be taken for granted that Theophylactus' chronology was correct and Sebeos' wrong.

Stein, however, favors the later date, explaining his preference
by the statement that Armenia was Persian before 590.[105] If this
means that Sebeos would not apply the term "Armenia" to any
part of the Roman dominion, it is erroneous. For Armenian
writers, "Armenia" was a national-geographic, not a political
designation.[106] Whether the territory, or any portion of it, de-
noted by that name was independent or whether it was subject to
some neighboring power, was to the Armenian author a matter of
indifference; for him it was always Armenia. The canton of Sper
(Ispir), for example, in the province of High Armenia was under
Maurice's jurisdiction.[107] Yet any Armenian author would certainly have described it as Armenia. It was the ancestral home of
the Bagratuni, one of whose members, Smbat, led the revolt.[108]

Siege of Dvin. Sebeos relates that John Mystacon laid siege to
Dvin, but, when Bahram revolted, abandoned the attack and went
ravaging Azerbaijan.[109] The event thus took place in 589. John
could not have begun the siege until the Armenian revolt had been
stamped out and until Bahram had retired into Albania. He abandoned it sometime in October.[110]

Battle of Nisibis. The sources quoted above for a fourfold invasion of Persia in the eleventh year of Hormisdas [111] include a

---

[104] Pp. 36-39.
[105] *Stud. z. Gesch. d. byz. Reiches*, p. 129.
[106] Hübschmann, *Altarm. Ortsn.*, pp. 216 f.
[107] *Ibid.*, pp. 245. 287.   [109] P. 13.
[108] *Ibid.*, p. 287.   [110] *Supra*, p. 36.
[111] *Supra*, p. 35, n. 88. The attack on Nisibis or an attack by the Romans
is mentioned in Dinawari, Tabari, Maqdisi, Masudi, Belami, Firdausi,
Nihayat and Mirkhond.

great attack on Nisibis, which can be only that of Comentiolus.[112] Hormisdas' eleventh year, however, ended July 2, 589, and the Roman expedition could not have been made so early. Evagrius states that, either when the battle was fought, or shortly afterwards, Bahram had already renounced his allegiance. From Theophylactus also, it is known that the usurper had taken up his position on the Zab only a very short time before the Persians suffered their great defeat in Syria.[113] As Bahram revolted after August 14, 589,[114] the authors that set Comentiolus' campaign previous to July 2 must be mistaken in the date. On the other hand, laying great insistence as they do upon the combination of perils that threatened Hormisdas from every side, they could easily have fallen into what is, after all, only a trifling error in chronology, while their point of view is entirely correct. The attack on Nisibis, though long delayed, was an integral part of Maurice's grand offensive of 589. It took place after August.

Capture of Acbas. Comentiolus took this fortress by storm just before winter.[115] At this time Bahram had slowly been advancing away from the Zab towards Ctesiphon and the crown.[116]

This completes the chronology of the events that raised Bahram to the throne of Persia, and attention may now be drawn to some difficulties that have so far been ignored. Baynes dates the fall of Martyropolis in 590 and the earthquake at Antioch in 589, arguing that Evagrius begins the Era of Antioch with October 1, 48 B. C.[117] In the first place, Chosroes fled in 590 and it is impossible to date the fall of Martyropolis in the same year. Secondly, with regard to the Era of Antioch, Evagrius gives July 9, 566 Era of Antioch for the accession of Justin I; [118] April 1, 575 for the proclamation of

---

[112] Theophyl. Sim. III 6, 1-4; Evagr. VI 15.

[113] IV 1, 2-7.   [114] *Supra*, p. 8.

[115] Evagr., *loc. cit.*; Theophyl. Sim. IV 2, 1.

[116] Theophyl. Sim., *loc. cit.*

[117] "The Literary Construction of the History of Theophylactus Simocatta," *Xénia, hommage international à l'Université Nationale de Grèce à l'occasion du soixante-quinzième anniversaire de sa fondation (1837-1912)* (Athens 1912), pp. 36 f.

[118] IV 1.

Justinian as Augustus;[119] November 561, sixth indiction, for the beginning of Severus' patriarchate;[120] September 567, first year of Justin I, for his flight from Antioch.[121] These dates correspond respectively to July 9, 518 A. D.;[122] April 1, 527 A. D.;[123] November 512 A. D. (since the sixth indiction was September 1. 512-13); September 518 A. D. (since Justin's first year was July 9, 518-19). In all these instances the era of Antioch is counted from 49 B. C. Since July 9, 518 A. D. is in 566 Era of Antioch, but September 518 A. D. in 567 Era of Antioch, the exact beginning of the Era of Antioch was September 1, 49 B. C. For any historian to be inconsistent in the use of an era seems very odd.

Evagrius' chronology presents another very serious difficulty; he prolongs the siege of Martyropolis for two years, 589-90. Only in the third, 591, does Bahram revolt, and, consequently, the coronation of Chosroes is moved into 592 and his restoration to 593.[124] This is out of the question. Romanus, who opposed Bahram in Suania,[125] went to Italy before January 591.[126] Furthermore Theophylactus makes it quite clear that the Persian revolt occurred in the same year as Martyropolis fell, not only negatively by omitting any of his usual references to the change of seasons, but positively, when he introduces his narrative of 589 by a detailed survey of the conditions throughout the Roman Empire—something that he does nowhere else.[127] This is evidently designed as a solemn prelude to the dramatic events whose unfolding was destined for the end of that year.

---

[119] IV 9.

[120] III 33.

[121] IV 4.

[122] *Cambridge Medieval History*, II 1.

[123] *Ibid.*, p. 2.

[124] VI 14.

[125] Theophyl. Sim. III 6, 17.

[126] GREGORII I PAPAE *registrum epistolarum* ed. P. Ewald and L. M. Hartmann, *MGH, epp. I-II* (Berlin 1887-99), I 20 (line 2). 44. This date is certain; that Romanus appeared in Italy as early as the end of 589, seems to be controverted.

[127] III 4, 6-9; cf. *infra*, pp. 57 f.

CHAPTER III

CHRONOLOGY FROM THE FLIGHT OF CHOSROES II, MARCH 1,
590, TO HIS RESTORATION, END OF 591

The chronology of this period of the Persian War presents more
difficulties and obscurities than any other. It is, therefore, best
to determine first the one date that can be fixed, that of the expedition of Zadespras, and then fill in the interval from Chosroes' flight
to that point.

Expedition of Zadespras. When Bahram learned that the Romans intended to back the ousted king with men and money, and
that the throne would have to be defended against them, he chose
Zadespras to hold the city of Nisibis, the key to the defense of the
west.[1] The new appointee, on departing from Ctesiphon to take
up his post, sent ahead his subordinates to announce his coming.
The leading men of Nisibis, however, having in the meantime been
won over to the cause of Chosroes,[2] seized these messengers. The
governor Solchanes, who had previously guaranteed that he would
win all Syria, now sent off Rosas at the head of some cavalry to
engage Zadespras.[3] For Chosroes, everything was cast in the bal-
ance. He vowed to St. Sergius, in the event of success, that he
would dedicate to him the first fruits of victory.[4] Almost within a
month he received the head of Zadespras.[5] When later he regained
his throne, he kept his word and attached to his offering an inscription in Greek.[6] This tells that the army under Rosas departed
on January 7 of his first year and the news of success came on
February 9; i. e., January 7 and February 9, 591.[7]

Postponement of Aid to Chosroes. Attention must be drawn to
a very striking feature of the above narrative: Zadespras had not
the slightest suspicion of conditions at Nisibis. On leaving Ctesiphon he dispatched messengers to announce his coming, thus fol-

---

[1] Theophyl. Sim. V 1, 1-3.
[2] *Ibid.*, IV 15, 7.
[3] *Ibid.*, V 1, 9.
[4] *Ibid.*, V 1, 6-8.
[5] *Ibid.*, V 2, 1.
[6] *Ibid.*, V 13, 4-6; Evagr. VI 21.
[7] Theophyl. Sim. V 13, 5; Evagr. VI 21.

lowing the ordinary procedure of any official going in security to his post of duty. Consequently, the defection of Nisibis had occurred so recently that it was still unknown to Bahram at Zadespras' departure. Further, Theophylactus expressly states that Bahram's appointment of Zadespras followed immediately upon his failure to win the good will of the Romans. In other words, the final decision of Maurice to restore the scion of the Sassanids to the throne of Persia and to refuse recognition to the usurper had been made known only a very brief time before January 7, 591. Yet, Chosroes had arrived on Roman territory in March 590. He had, therefore, to wait a long while for the formal promise of aid from his host.

The existence of this considerable interval is demonstrated by chronological hints scattered throughout the sources. Belami, for instance, says that Bahram reigned at Ctesiphon for a year.[8] Again, there is a story of how Chosroes in the early stages of his residence in Roman territory encountered a hermit who predicted, according to various versions, either that his restoration would begin twelve months thence, or that it would be completed within seventeen or eighteen months, or again within seventeen months and eighteen days.[9] Mirkhond, in fact, gives eighteen months as the length of Chosroes' sojourn in Roman territory.[10] Firdausi, however, is most explicit; for he has the Emperor make profuse apologies for the postponement of the promised aid and ascribes it to the necessity of mustering his demobilized armies.[11]

Finally, though Theophylactus might seem, on superficial reading, to contradict the above evidence, yet, a close examination of his narrative serves rather to confirm it. Thus he relates that at the beginning of spring 590 [12] Chosroes sent a formal embassy to Constantinople, which presented his case so convincingly to the Senate that the whole might of Rome was immediately placed at his disposal.[13] On the other hand, the ambassador, in the course of the speech attributed to him by the historian, alludes to the fact that Bahram had also sent envoys to make counterproposals.[14] Of these

---

[8] II 280; from March 590 to March 591, though, as a matter of fact, Bahram does not seem to have left Ctesiphon until the summer of 591; cf. Theophyl. Sim. V 4, 2 and *vide infra* p. 53.

[9] Fird. VII 78; Bel. II 289; Nih., p. 239.

[10] P. 398.   [11] VII 90. 107.   [12] IV 13, 3.   [13] IV 14, 1 f.   [14] IV 13, 20.

negotiations Theophylactus gives the detail further on.[15]   Directly
upon Chosroes' reception, Maurice had informed the usurper that
he had lent a favorable ear to the refugee's request.   In answer to
this official notice Bahram in turn dispatched his representatives to
offer the surrender of Nisibis and its environs as the price of neu-
trality.   To this offer there is a plain reference in the speech of
Chosroes' ambassador.   He contrasts its extravagance with the
reasonableness of his own proposals and points out that the ac-
ceptance of so great a piece of Persian territory would inevitably
defeat the whole aim of Maurice's policy, a permanent peace on a
basis of mutual fair play.[16]   This proves that Theophylactus takes
occasion of the embassy's arrival in the capital to present the reasons
back of Maurice's whole policy.   The speech is a rhetorical device.
It sums up the result of deliberations that actually took months, and
the author intended, beyond any doubt, that his context should show
this.[17]

He furnishes other indications equally unmistakable; this time,
in his description of Bindoes' activities, who, as has been mentioned,
accompanied the king on his flight but was recaptured and brought
back two days before Bahram's coronation, March 7, 590.[18]   Chosroes
apparently was detained at Hierapolis for the duration of the negotiations at Constantinople, and was permitted only after the final
decision had been reached in his favor to take up his residence in
the border city, Constantina, whence he could easily keep in touch
with his own subjects.[19]   But even before his departure from Hierapolis he sent Bestam into Armenia to win him support there.[20]
Meantime Bindoes, who was Bestam's brother, escaped from prison,
made his way to Azerbaijan, and ten days after his arrival got in

---

[15] IV 14, 8 f.

[16] IV 13, 25. Note, too, the attention given otherwise to Bahram's pro-
posal and the space given to it in the speech, IV, 13, 20-23.

[17] The whole matter will be fully discussed in Part II of this work.
There is no doubt that Theophylactus glosses over the controversy between
Maurice and the Senate; cf. Seb., p. 15; John Nik. 96, 11-13; Yaq. I 191;
Din., p. 96; Bel. II 290 f.; Fird. VII 86-90; Agap. Hier. *PO* VIII 444. But
however false the impression he thus produces, he does not distort the
chronology.

[18] *Supra*, p. 30.   [19] IV 14, 5.   [20] IV 12, 10.

touch with John Mystacon, the *magister militum per Armeniam*.[21] John detained his messenger while he inquired of Maurice the proper procedure. Just one day before Bestam's arrival, John received the answer to support Bindoes with all the means at his disposal. This last is an extremely important detail. It shows beyond any doubt that the Emperor's highest military official in Armenia had not yet had time to learn of the final decision in Chosroes' case. Though the exact length of Bindoes' imprisonment cannot be determined, it was certainly not short. Not only is this the general impression conveyed by the narrative of other sources,[22] but Firdausi explicitly puts his term at seventy days [23] and Belami at three or four months.[24] Furthermore, just before Bindoes' escape Bahram had received a contingent of barbarian mercenaries.[25] These could only be Turks.[26] Whether the usurper had actually made a solemn treaty with their Chagan or not, the presence of these mercenaries presupposes a very considerable interval after his coronation.

Chosroes, therefore, did not receive aid from Maurice immediately, but waited long for the ultimate decision, until November or December 590 perhaps; at least, no more allowance need be made before the dispatch of Rosas on January 7, 591. Meantime, Bindoes had been held captive for the greater part of the year but made his way to Azerbaijan at about the same time that Maurice finally gave his assent to Chosroes' proposals.

---

[21] IV 14, 9–IV 15, 5.

[22] Din., pp. 94 f.; Tab. Nöld., p. 282; Eut. *MPG* 57, 717 B; Bel. II 282-84; Fird. VII 64-69.

[23] VII 64.

[24] II 282. 283. Firdausi frequently has such variations in the figures; cf. *supra*, p. 43. It is impossible to decide how accurate Belami is, as there is no way of determining how long it took Bindoes to gain safety in Azerbaijan. At least, he conveys the notion of a long imprisonment.

[25] Theophyl. Sim. IV 14, 13.

[26] Seb., pp. 12 f. (All the sources dependent on the *Khvadhaynamagh* place the revolt of Bahram immediately after his victory over the Turks and omit all reference to the invasion of Suania; cf. Nöldeke, Tab., pp. 272 f., n. 3.) Mas. II 217, quoted from an Arab poet; Yaq. I 190; Thaal., p. 658; Tab., Nöld., pp. 274. 280; Bel. II 292 f.; Fird. VI 553 f.; VII 31 f. 40. 41. 43. 58 f. (Chazar king prominent in debate before Bahram's coronation); Theophyl. Sim. V 10, 13-15.

Surrender of Martyropolis. Even after Chosroes had taken refuge with the Romans, Martyropolis at his express orders still held out, but he was forced ultimately to yield it back to Maurice.[27] The surrender can be dated roughly by the fact that Dometianus was mainly responsible for its recovery. Since he joined the Persian king at Constantina,[28] and since, as has just been seen, Chosroes came to that city only after the final decision in his favor, the siege of the fortress must have lasted, at least, until December 590.

How much longer it is impossible to say. Theophylactus, it is true, completes this portion of his narrative before taking up the expedition of Rosas from Nisibis, which would imply that the recapture occurred before January 7, 591. Though, on the whole, he follows a strictly chronological order in his history, still he occasionally abandons it without warning the reader (as in the instance just discussed where he completes the account of the negotiations between Maurice and Chosroes and then goes back to pick up the simultaneous events in Persia and Armenia). There is no guarantee that he has not done something similar with the siege of Martyropolis. On the other hand, Evagrius' narrative seems to insinuate that he has; at least, no other explanation suggests itself for the extraordinary error to which attention has already been called.[29] After telling of the betrayal of the fortress in 589, the *Ecclesiastical History* details the vain efforts made to storm it and asserts that the assaulters went into winter quarters; that, in the following summer, i. e., 590, they fought the battle in which Mebodes lost his life; that, after a second winter, that is, in 591,[30] Philippicus gave over the command to Comentiolus;[31] and finally, that Chosroes, upon leaving Hierapolis, tendered Martyropolis to his benefactor, presumably in 592.[32] This confusion by which the events of 589 are spread over three years is difficult to explain in a contemporary writer. It can, however, be better understood if, as a matter of

---

[27] Theophyl. Sim. IV 12, 9; IV 13, 1; IV 15, 8 ff. Theophylactus' narrative, the most detailed and reliable, is here followed to the exclusion of the others, whose variations will be treated in Part II of the present work.

[28] *Ibid.*, IV 14, 5.

[29] *Supra*, p. 41.

[30] VI 14; pp. 232, lines 20. 23; p. 233, lines 2 f. Bidez and Parmentier.

[31] VI 15.   [32] VI 19.

fact, the investment of Martyropolis lasted through two winters and well into the third, until February or March 591. The following information may also be some guide to the duration of the siege. Dometianus, as a memorial of the city's deliverance, instituted a new feast of the martyrs in whose honor it had been named; [33] these were the Persian Christians put to death under Sapor II.[34] They were commemorated on February 16 in the East.[35] Whether the date has anything to do with Dometianus' rededication of Martyropolis, the present writer cannot say. Since an adequate treatment of the question involving an investigation of the whole history of the feast would carry this dissertation too far outside its province, it has not been attempted. The date would, however, agree well enough with Evagrius' narrative as interpreted above.

Proclamation of Chosroes at Mardes (Marde, Mardin). Directly after the expedition against Zadespras, at the beginning of spring 591, Chosroes finally left Constantina for Mardes.[36] This marks the real start of his march back to his domain. It was signalized by an impressive ceremony. All the nobles from Nisibis and its environs, the high civil and military officials, the notables and dignitaries of the whole region gathered here. These together with the lords that had shared the hardships and perils of the flight once more proclaimed him king. They solemnly pledged their oath to set him again on the throne of his fathers. For an earnest of their loyalty, they surrendered their relatives as hostages, and Chosroes transferred them to the safekeeping of the Roman soldiers.

This event is of great significance for the chronology because it seems to have been the determining factor in the reckoning of the western Syriac writers. This at least appears the proper interpretation of a passage in Michael Syrus, that the Persians revolted against Hormisdas in the eighth year of Maurice, but, at the end

---

[33] Theophyl. Sim. IV 15, 18.

[34] J. Labourt, *Le Christianisme dans l'Empire Perse sous la dynastie sassanide (224-632)* (2nd ed., Paris 1904) (*Bibliothèque de l'enseignement de l'histoire ecclésiastique*), p. 89.

[35] Hippolytus Delehaye, S. J., *Synaxarium Ecclesiae Const. . . . (Propylaeum ad Acta SS. Nov.*, Brussels 1902), p. 469.

[36] Theophyl. Sim. V 3, 1-3.

of ten months, in the ninth year of Maurice, Chosroes was elected king.[37] Hormisdas was dethroned on February 6, 590, a date on which all sources agree with the Syriac chronicler;[38] but what can he mean by the statement that a successor was not chosen until considerably later? To what event can he refer so pointedly for the beginning of the reign of Chosroes? The date, ten months after the putting aside of Hormisdas, would be in December, about the time that the Senate agreed to the restoration of the exiled king. This is not impossible as the moment at which to fix the real accession.

Despite the fact, however, that this interpretation of the passage fits so nicely into the conclusions drawn from the narrative of Theophylactus, still, so obscure and indirect a condition to success as the sanction of Maurice's project by his advisers, however essential it might be, hardly strikes one as a satisfactory milestone in Chosroes' career at which to date his inauguration. But the proclamation at Mardes was something definite and tangible; it was a brilliant day in the young prince's life; it was the solemn occasion on which he became once more king in his own right, clothed in royal raiment, attended by obsequious courtiers, surrounded by an enthusiastic army. Moreover, it took place in the very heart of the Syriac district, hard by Nisibis; it was the Syriac population that had supported him in his exile;[39] it was their loyalty that had given him his first right to hope in the dark days at Constantina; and it was their day, as well as his, when the world again hailed him as king at Mardes.

It need cause no surprise, therefore, if this day impressed itself on the pages of western Syriac history. Though it was much more than ten months after the deposition of Hormisdas, it must be the time from which both Michael Syrus and his source dated the beginning of Chosroes' reign. The figure is only a trifling objection to this view. It arose, presumably, from some mistaken notion that the proclamation at Mardes followed hard upon the sanction of the Senate—a confusion which is, in the light of all the circumstances,

---

[37] II 360.   [38] *Supra*, p. 26.

[39] This question of Syriac support is to be discussed in Part III of the present work; cf. Theophyl. Sim. V 1, 13, where Rosas' spy gains instant admittance to Zadespras merely by speaking Persian.

and particularly if one consider the scantness of the chronicler generally, very easy to understand. But the all-important and vital feature of the statement is that it makes a clear-cut and unmistakable distinction between the revolt against Hormisdas and the accession of his son. Furthermore, let it be emphasized that while it sets the former action in the eighth year of Maurice—and, in this, all sources agree with it however independent the tradition each represents—yet, unlike them, it gives a date in the following year for the beginning of Chosroes' reign. This passage also explains the chronology of other writers of the locality. James of Edessa [40] and Elias of Nisibis, who probably relies upon him,[41] both date the accession of Chosroes in 902 Sel., i. e., October 1, 590-91.

Upon this explanation there should be two methods of computing Chosroes' regnal years, which according to the Persian system, ought to begin with the New Year's Day previous to his accession. The normal count would be from July 2, 589, the western Syriac from June 27, 590. To test this hypothesis properly would lead to an investigation of the whole chronology of his reign and bring the present work too far afield, but some examples may here be cited in support of the view. Thus, whereas the majority of writers assign him thirty-eight years—and this is correct almost to the day (February 15, 590 to February 25, 628)—Elias gives him only thirty-seven.[42] Sebeos always reckons from 589, as the following citations

[40] *Chronicon* JACOBI EDESSENI *interpretatus est* E. W. Brooks, *CSCO, scr. Syri, III, 4, Chr. min.* (Rome, Paris and Leipzig 1905), p. 246.

[41] Nöldeke, Tab., p. 430; cf. ELIAE *metropolitae* NISIBENI *opus chronologicum (Pars prior) interpretatus est* E. W. Brooks, *CSCO, scr. Syri, III, 7* (Rome, Paris, and Leipzig 1910), p. 60; *ibid.*, n. 1, the source is probably James of Edessa.

[42] P. 26; cf. Nöldeke, Tab., p. 432. Among those who give thirty-seven years Nöldeke here cites Sebeos. Sebeos, however, never mentions the length of Chosroes' reign, and, in fact, gives no regnal years after his thirty-fourth (p. 79). The figure thirty-seven comes from Pseudo-Sebeos; cf. *Journal Asiatique*[10] 6 (1905) 149. Nöldeke, as can be gathered from Tab., pp. vi; 269, n. 1; 272 ff., n. 3, relied for his knowledge of Sebeos on Patkanian; cf. Évariste Prud'homme, " Essai d'une histoire de la dynastie des Sassanides, d'après les renseignements fournis par les historiens arméniens, par M. K. Patkanian: traduit du russe," *Journal Asiatique*[6] 7 (1866) 101-238. Since this article (p. 192, n. 1) quotes Sebeos as the authority for the fact that Chosroes II came to the throne in Maurice's seventh year, a

prove: Maurice's death (November 602) in Chosroes' fourteenth year; [43] Heraclius' first year (October 5, 610-11) begins in Chosroes' twenty-second; [44] the capture of Jerusalem is on Margatz 27 (?), of Chosroes' twenty-fifth year.[45] As Sebeos' work depends intimately on Persian sources, his testimony is of great importance in settling the chronology of Chosroes' reign.[46] The western Syriac reckoning, on the other hand, is followed exclusively by Michael Syrus.[47]

With all these facts established, it is now possible to examine critically the views of Nöldeke and Bury, each of whom independently and on entirely different grounds arrived at the same conclusion, viz., that Chosroes II was crowned late in 590. Nöldeke in his study of the chronology of the Sassanids, based predominantly on Oriental sources, fixed the date of his accession very shortly after the Persian New Year's Day of 590.[48] He argues that: 1. According to the subscription of a contemporary Syriac codex, the tenth year of Chosroes II coincided with 911 Sel. and this makes the first year roundly equivalent to 902 Sel., October 1, 590-91; 2. This contemporary subscription is confirmed by the authority of Elias of Nisibis, by the *Anonymous of 724*,[49] and the *Chronicon paschale*;

statement found only in Pseudo-Sebeos, *supra*, p. 28, it proves that Patkanian makes no distinction between the two, and accounts for Nöldeke's citation referred to above. Pseudo-Sebeos, though he gives the correct date for Chosroes' accession, probably calculated the brief reigns of his successors wrongly, and this accounts for the thirty-seven years assigned to Chosroes without making it necessary to suppose that he derived the information from western Syriac sources. (As at the present time there are reliable translations of all the Armenian sources quoted by Patkanian for this period, it is no longer necessary to use his article for them.)

[43] P. 55.   [44] P. 64.

[45] P. 68. Margatz is the eleventh month of the Armenian calendar.

[46] This is proved in Part II of the present work.

[47] II 400-13 *passim*.   [48] Tab., pp. 430 f.

[49] Quoted by Nöldeke from Land; cf. *Chronicon miscellaneum ad annum domini 724 pertinens interpretatus est* J.-B. Chabot, *CSCO, scr. Syri III 4, Chr. min.* (Rome, Paris, and Leipzig 1904), p. 112. The entry gives two dates, 902 Sel. and ind. IX. The former begins October 1, the latter September 1; cf. *ibid.*, p. 111, Severus was expelled from Antioch (*vide supra*, p. 41) Elul 29, 829 Sel., ind. XII. September 29, 518 is in ind. XII, which began September 1, 518 and in 829 Sel., if it ended October 1, 518. As Chabot points out, the book is a compilation and uses at times a Greek

3. Since the dedicatory inscriptions show both January 7, and February 9, 591 in his first year, he could not have come to the throne before the previous New Year's Day, June 27, 590.

It is at once obvious that these reasons present a very powerful case in favor of Nöldeke's findings and raise most serious objections to the results of this dissertation; but over against them can be set all the evidence so far adduced for the chronology adopted in this study. The pivotal date is March 9 for the coronation of Bahram. Conclusive proofs for its correctness have been marshalled above.[50] It is, therefore, a fact that Chosroes came to the throne before March 590, and the question comes down to this: how can that fact be reconciled with the passages cited by Nöldeke?

Elias of Nisibis has been satisfactorily interpreted in the previous discussion, and the *Chronicon paschale* will be treated below. This leaves the two contemporary records for present consideration.

As has been mentioned repeatedly, the Persian kings counted their regnal years from the New Year's previous to their accession, and if January 7, 591 is in the first year of Chosroes II, it ought to mean that he was crowned after June 27, 590. But his accession really occurred February 15, 590. Did he abandon an immemorial custom and adopt for his reign the Roman practise? This is not to be thought of and is mentioned only to be dismissed. His immediate successor followed the normal Sassanid usage,[51] and for Chosroes to have made capriciously so revolutionary a change seems too great an anomaly to be worth serious consideration. Another explanation is preferable: he saw fit to employ a foreign turn of expression in the document attached to the votive offering. After all, it was in Greek that the dedication was written; it was in the months and days of the Greek, not the Persian calendar, that the events were described; a Greek-reading public was to receive information from the inscription; and it does not seem difficult to suppose that for these reasons he preferred a chronological terminology that was native to the language he borrowed and familiar to the people for whom the

source employed also by *Chronicon paschale*. For the notice of Chosroes' flight, the text itself and the indiction come from the Greek original, while the Seleucid year derives from a western Syriac source. The *Anonymous of 724*, then, adds nothing to the adverse evidence.

[50] *Supra*, pp. 8 ff.   [51] Nöldeke, Tab., p. 432.

declaration was intended. After all, by far the majority of Roman subjects would not have understood him if he had written " January 7 in his second year "; it was a mode of reckoning strange to them and would have served only to cast suspicion on the document in the eyes of many who knew from other sources the time at which the benefits acknowledged in it had been received.

As for the Syriac codex, there is no solution save to suppose that an error has been made somewhere, either by Wright[52] in his description of the manuscript, or by the author of the colophon. The scribe might, in this instance, have inadvertently written 911 Sel. and 10 Chosroes instead of 910 Sel. and 11 Chosroes.

Bury[53] also dates the accession of Chosroes after September 590. Inasmuch as he does not cite Tabari,[54] and, for the material derived from the Persian and Arabic sources, makes acknowledgment only to Rawlinson,[55] it may be presumed that he drew his conclusions independently of Nöldeke, and that the principal authority for his chronology is the *Chronicon paschale*.[56] This work contains but the scantiest information on the whole of Maurice's reign, but it does notice under the ninth indiction (September 1, 590-91) and the seventh post-consulate of Maurice (December 25, 590-91) that Chosroes was expelled by Bahram and brought back by the Romans. Assuredly, if the terseness of the *Chronicon's* entries for this period be considered, it is easy to understand that the author decided not to distribute over two years this meagre memorandum but simply to note it under the one year, 591, in which the Romans exercised their principal activity in Chosroes' behalf. It hardly constitutes a serious objection to Theophylactus' detailed, careful account of the entire history of Bahram's rebellion and Chosroes' restoration. For that matter Bury himself probably attributed to it no such overwhelming authority. In a pioneer work of the breadth of his *Later Roman Empire* he could patently not devote a penetrating study to such minutiae as to whether Chosroes fled in March or September 590.

---

[52] *Catalogue of the Syriac Manuscripts in the British Museum, Acquired Since the Year 1838* (London 1870-72), I 52 f.

[53] *Later Roman Empire*, II 111.

[54] He is not mentioned among the sources used; cf. *ibid.*, p. 83, n. 1.

[55] *Ibid.*, pp. 111, n. 1; 112, n. 1.　　　　[56] P. 691 Bonn.

Chosroes' Campaign Against Bahram and Final Victory. The
proclamation of Chosroes at Mardes took place in the spring as
has just been seen; it was followed shortly afterwards by the surrender of Dara to the Romans.[57] Agapius [58] remarks that the city
had been in the hands of the Persians for seventeen years, and, as
Chosroes I had captured it on November 11 or 15, 573,[59] this agrees
sufficiently with the date of spring 591 for its restoration. It was
not, however, until the beginning of summer that the combined
armies under Chosroes and Narses finally started out against
Bahram.[60] For the duration of the expedition the only exact information is the statement of Agapius [61] that it lasted until the end
of 902 Sel., i. e., until October 1, 591. The rest of the sources
seem, on the whole, to support him. Theophylactus' account of the
campaign, again, is the most accurate and detailed. There were
two phases. As Bahram had planned not to shut himself in Ctesiphon but to decide the issue in open battle, Chosroes dispatched
Mebodes to seize the capital,[62] while, with the main body of the
troops, he advanced towards Adiabene to engage the rebel. Mebodes
went first to Singaron to put the king's harem in a secure place,[63]
marched down the Euphrates, and succeeded in mastering the whole
complex of cities around Ctesiphon. The messengers of the victory
overtook Chosroes only very shortly after the king had gone across
the mountains into Azerbaijan.[64] This means that the movements
of Narses [65] before ever he fought a single pitched battle with
Bahram consumed a very considerable time. To determine it more
precisely there are only two indications. The Roman plan was for
Narses to march from Syria and John Mystacon from Armenia,
to trap Bahram between them. According to Theophylactus,[66]
Bahram, while he was still maneuvering on the Zab, began to hope
that the junction, because of the difficulty of the terrain, never
would be made. Presumably, since Mystacon had to use the Keli-

[57] Theophyl. Sim. V 3, 10.
[58] *PO* VIII 446.
[59] Stein, *Stud. z. Gesch. d. byz. Reiches*, p. 46.
[60] Theophyl. Sim. V 4, 3.
[61] *PO* VIII 447.
[62] V 4, 2.
[63] V 4, 1 f.
[64] V 9, 1.
[65] V 5, 4–V 6, 1; V 7, 10–V 8, 10.
[66] V 8, 3.

5

Shin to come into Adiabene, it would soon have been too late for him to get over the pass; in other words, it was already towards the beginning of autumn.[67] Firdausi,[68] furthermore, says that Chosroes took two months to reach Azerbaijan from the Byzantine territory. On the basis of this information, one may, with sufficient assurance, date the final battles with Bahram and the end of the long war between Persia and Rome in September 591.[69]

[67] *Supra*, p. 36.

[68] VII 112.

[69] Bury, " The Chronology of Theophylaktos Simokatta," *English Historical Review*, 3 (1888) 311, expresses a different view, but Baynes, *Xénia*, p. 39, proves it untenable.

CHAPTER IV

CHRONOLOGY FROM THE ACCESSION OF MAURICE,
AUGUST 14, 582, TO THE MUTINY, 588

The chronology from the mutiny in Syria to the final restoration
of Chosroes having been studied, attention may now be given to the
previous years from the accession of Maurice (August 14, 582) to
the mutiny of 588. This completes the chronology of the Persian
War in his reign.

Battle of Solachon. It is necessary first to fix the date of the
battle at Solachon, the great victory of the Roman general Philippicus. As will be seen, Theophylactus' chronology offers some difficulty because it is capable of various interpretations, but, fortunately, the testimony of another source is unequivocal. This is
John of Ephesus.[1] Though the incomplete manuscript of his *Ecclesiastical History* breaks off in 894 Sel. (October 1, 582-83)[2] one
heading in the table of contents to the sixth book refers to a battle
in the third year that resulted in a triumph for the Roman side.[3]
This is undoubtedly the engagement at Solachon in which the
Persian army was almost annihilated. The third year must be that
of Maurice, August 14, 584-85.[4] Of this date, we find a confirmation in John of Biclar.[5] In his *Chronicle* he states that in the third
year of Maurice, the Emperor attacked the Persians through his
commanders. As the war had already lasted since 572,[6] it is only
natural to suppose that this special mention of the hostilities refers
to some event quite out of the ordinary, and the wording implies

---

[1] *Die Kirchengeschichte des* JOHANNES VON EPHESUS *aus dem Syrischen
übersetzt, mit einer Abhandlung über die Tritheiten von* J. M. Schönfelder
(Munich 1862).

[2] *Ibid.*, VI 37.   [3] *Ibid.*, VI 44.

[4] In confirmation of this interpretation, note Anton Baumstark's remark
that the *Church History* relates events to 585; cf. *Geschichte der syrischen
Literatur mit Ausschluss der christlich-palästinensischen Texte* (Bonn
1922), p. 182.

[5] *Chr. min.* (*MGH, auct. ant., XI*), II 217.

[6] Stein, *Stud. z. Gesch. d. byz. Reiches*, p. 25.

that it is a Roman victory. The conclusion is thus borne out that Solachon was fought in 585.

Before discussing the chronology of Theophylactus, his historical terminology and method must be considered. It is only rarely and in isolated instances that he gives an actual calendar date, such as December 7 for the promotion of Tiberius.[7] In imitation of the practise of the classical historians, he marks the progress of time by the device of indicating the change of seasons. He usually opens his account of the military campaigns with a mention of spring and closes it with the remark that the army went into winter quarters,[8] though occasionally and for some special reason he may refer to summer or autumn. In the course of his narrative he should be expected, then, normally to use the word "year," not in the sense of the accepted divisions of the calendar, running from January to January, or (the regular Byzantine practise) from September to September, but rather of the military season that started in spring.

An instance is the meaning of "year" in the following episode. The Chagan of the Avars, after suddenly attacking Singidunum in summer when the harvest had just ripened,[9] ravaged his way right up to the environs of Anchialus,[10] where, three months later, he received envoys from the Emperor.[11] The negotiations proving unsuccessful, Maurice again dispatched an embassy in the following year.[12] A study of these data proves that "in the following year" cannot mean "in the following September" but only "in the following spring." The barbarians opened their campaign at the moment when the people were gathering the crops, i. e., at the earliest, in the third week of June, if it were barley, or in the last week, if it were wheat.[13] The next indication "three months"

---

[7] III 11, 13.

[8] *Vide* II 10, 5 f. for a very characteristic example.

[9] I 4, 2.   [10] I 4, 3-5.   [11] I 4, 6.   [12] I 6, 4.

[13] The Danubian Valley is on the same isotherm as Kansas in the United States, and wheat in that State is ripe enough to harvest at the earliest by June 23; barley comes in about a week sooner. The Foreign Agricultural Service of the U. S. Department of Agriculture was kind enough to examine for the writer its reports from Belgrade, and their information agrees very closely with the foregoing, though the harvest in the Danubian Valley often comes in much later than that of Kansas, due to greater variation in the climate.

causes the same trouble that has already been met.[14] Does it mean after the attack on Singidunum or after that on Anchialus? Even if it be supposed that the harvest mentioned in Theophylactus was barley, nevertheless, three months added to the third week of June give a date later than the beginning of September. In addition, the historian inserts the journey of the envoys to and from Anchialus and their dealings with the Chagan between his mention of the harvest and his statement about the " following year." It is hardly possible in this context to apply the phrase to the following September 1. It is clear, then, that " the following year " is not that which ran from September to September, but rather the season fit for military operations. In confirmation of this be it noted that Theophylactus in the sequel omits any mention of spring as being implicit in the phrase " the following year " and consequently unnecessary. He continues simply with a reference to summer [15] and autumn.[16]

A further instance is his statement that Monocarton had been fortified by Philippicus " in the past year." [17] This general had taken up his duties in autumn [18] and had made two rapid thrusts into Persian territory.[19] . " In the following year," [20] he invaded Arzanene but had to cease active campaigning because of illness.[21] During his incapacity Monocarton was attacked, but in vain,[22] as he had had the foresight to strengthen its defenses " in the past year." What can the " past year " be? Theophylactus has indicated autumn as the time of Philippicus' arrival. By the words " in the following year," he must mean the following spring. Since the autumn had been crowded with activity, the only leisure time available for work on Monocarton's repair could have been the winter before the spring campaign. It is to that winter alone that he can refer by the words " in the previous year." This demonstrates again that spring begins the year, not September or January.

The same concept of " year " is unmistakably suggested in the passage already cited [23] in which he summarizes the general conditions at the beginning of 589.[24] He has just told how the Roman

---

[14] *Supra*, p. 29.   [18] I 13, 3.   [22] I 14, 6.

[15] I 7, 5.   [19] I 13, 4-12.   [23] *Supra*, p. 41.

[16] I 8, 1.   [20] I 14, 1.   [24] III 4, 6-9.

[17] I 14, 6.   [21] I 14, 5.

mutineers, returning from a foray into enemy territory, turned on
their Persian pursuers at Martyropolis and practically annihilated
them.[25]   At this point, by the mention of winter and spring, he
marks the transition from 588 to 589.[26]   Next he pauses to present
a picture of military conditions throughout the Empire, on the
eastern front, in the Balkans, in Italy, and in Africa.   Above all,
he lays emphasis on the profound peace that reigned in Lazica.[27]
This stress prepares the reader to understand the events in the
Caucasus.   Later in the year Bahram invaded Suania,[28] and Theophylactus, again calling special attention to the long quiet that
had obtained there,[29] explains thus the total unpreparedness of the
Romans.   The obvious position in the narrative for such introductory matter would be at the beginning of the year in which the
events took place.   Since Theophylactus does not place it after a
mention of autumn or winter to correspond to a year from September 1 or January 1, but only after he has marked the arrival of
spring, it shows that the word " year " suggested to him, naturally
and almost subconsciously, the season fit for military operations.
This is all the more surprising because the very words with which
he begins his account of Bahram's invasion are: " It was the eighth
year of the reign of the Emperor Maurice, and Bahram . . . " [30]
This would certainly seem the logical point at which to pause for
a review of conditions in general, especially when in that review
the author stresses the particular circumstances that made the foray
possible and effective.   Yet, he does not; and the only reason can
be that he did not view the regnal years as chronological divisions
at all.   They are points in time, not periods of it.   The only real
year runs from spring to spring, and the regnal year means no more
than any other single date.   He might as well have written,
August 14.

Before proceeding with the chronology it is indispensable here
to digress and to investigate one aspect of Theophylactus' method
of composition, the general discussion of the subject being reserved
to Part II of the present work.   The feature that is of importance

[25] III 4, 1-3; III 5, 8.
[26] III 4, 6.
[27] III 4, 7-9.

[28] *Supra*, p. 36.
[29] III 6, 7 f.
[30] *Ibid.*

has already been ably analyzed by Adamek.[31] He proves by a comparison with Theophanes Confessor that both the historian and the chronicler made independent use of some source that gave particular attention to events at Constantinople and within the circle of the royal family. It was from this that Theophylactus derived such items as the fire in the Forum,[32] the earthquake at Constantinople,[33] and the consulship of Maurice.[34]

Adamek pushes the conclusion no farther. If, however, Theophylactus compiled his work from various authorities, unless he dovetailed them with the utmost skill, traces would still remain where the joints were made. The joints, in fact, do show. Baynes calls attention [35] to the clumsy way in which is introduced the general summary of conditions at the beginning of 589.[36] *After* the victory at Martyropolis Theophylactus comes into a new year, 589, and prefaces his account with a review of the military state of the Empire. Then he continues, " Just at this time was brought to maturity a deed not unworthy of the pages of this book," and he tells a stirring tale of how those captured in Dara broke from their prison in the heart of Persia and fought their way home.[37] For fear, however, that his arrangement might be misleading, he takes care to caution the reader that they arrived in Roman territory just *before* the battle at Martyropolis.[38] This is an extraordinary inconsistency. The narrative begins with the statement that the escape occurred after the spring of 589 and ends with the assertion that it took place before the winter of 588. How explain this? Suppose the general summary be omitted. The reader can see the result of the omission best by reading the text of Theophylactus for himself, but the following paraphrase gives an idea of the effect: The Romans turned on the Persians at Martyropolis and won an overwhelming victory; at this time a brilliant achievement of the Romans in Persia came to an end; the prisoners taken at Dara

---

[31] *Beiträge zur Geschichte des byzantinischen Kaisers Mauricius (582-602) (Jahresbericht des ersten k. k. Staats-Gymnasiums in Graz*, Graz, 1890), pp. 25 f.

[32] I 11, 1 f.

[33] I 12, 8-11.

[34] I 12, 12 f.

[35] *Xénia*, pp. 35 f. 37.

[36] *Supra*, pp. 57 f.

[37] III 5, 1-7.

[38] III 5, 8.

escaped and after many an adventure returned to Roman territory; this outstanding triumph occurred while the battle at Martyropolis, which Theophylactus has previously described, was still in preparation. The account as thus outlined is now quite consistent and logical. The words "at this time" refer to the victory at Martyropolis. Furthermore, it is natural enough for Theophylactus to finish the story of the victory before introducing the episode of the prisoners' arrival, and to correct the false impression he might thus produce. The above was most likely the first draft of the composition. Later he thrust in the general summary before the words "at this time." This insertion produced the distortion in the narrative as it was finally left.

These preliminary considerations will lead to a better understanding of Theophylactus' chronology from 582 to 585. He relates that Maurice immediately upon his succession appointed John Mystacon *magister militum per orientem,* and that a battle was fought on the Nymphius in autumn, i. e., of 582.[39] Then follows a series of miscellaneous events, the marriage of the Emperor,[40] the fire in the Forum,[41] the incident of Paulinus,[42] a second campaign of Mystacon,[43] and the earthquake at Constantinople.[44] Theophylactus himself fixes the fire in the Forum at the beginning of spring, and the earthquake at its height. Theophanes gives the month of April[45] for the one, and May 10, 583,[46] for the other. The incidents seem clearly to be given in their chronological order. The second campaign of Mystacon began between April and May 10, 583. It consisted mainly of an unsuccessful attack on Acbas. Of the correctness of this information independent evidence is furnished by John of Ephesus according to whom the citadel was besieged in 894 Sel., i. e., October 1, 582-83.[47]

So far, then, the chronology is clear enough. Theophylactus next indicates the second year of Maurice and the assumption therein of the consulship.[48] He then proceeds: "In this current year,"

[39] I 9, 4-11.   [41] I 11, 1 f.   [43] I 12, 1-7.
[40] I 10, 1-12.   [42] I 11, 3-21.   [44] I 12, 8-11.
[45] THEOPHANIS *chronographia,* ed. by C. de Boor (Leipzig 1883), p. 252, 27.
[46] P. 252, 29.
[47] VI 37; cf. Mich. Syr. II 360.   [48] I 12, 12 f.

Philippicus replaced John Mystacon [49] and took up his new duties
at the beginning of autumn.[50] In the following year [51] he invaded
Arzanene and in winter went to Constantinople.[52] Upon his return in spring,[53] some unsatisfactory overtures of peace being rejected,[54] he prepared for battle. During the same year he won the
decisive victory of Solachon.[55] Now, as proved above, this conflict
is dated in 585 by two historians of the day who were independent
both of each other and of Theophylactus.[56] All three would agree
if Philippicus' appointment came in autumn 583, his invasion of
Arzanene in spring 584, his journey to Constantinople at the end
of 584, his return to his post in the spring of 585. Can such a
chronology fit Theophylactus' narrative? Maurice entered upon
his consulship in winter of his second year, more precisely December
25, 583,[57] and Theophylactus says that in this current year, apparently Maurice's second, i. e., August 14, 583-84, Philippicus
replaced John Mystacon, but did not arrive at his new post until
autumn. The historian seems to have followed up to this point
a strictly chronological order. Because the autumn of 583 was over
before the assumption of the consulship, he would naturally be
presumed to refer to the autumn of 584. The passage would then
mean that Philippicus received his appointment before August 14,
584, but actually took up his duties only in autumn 584. To such
a chronology objections can be raised even on the basis of the context. It would have to be supposed that nothing noteworthy occurred from the battle of Acbas in spring 583 to the autumn of 584,
a period of eighteen months. Though the inherent improbability
of so long a cessation of hostilities might not be enough to justify
the rejection of this chronology, still it is sufficient to rouse suspicion, and when confirmed by extrinsic evidence certainly suggests
a re-examination of the text on which it is based.

As a matter of fact, the narrative of Theophylactus viewed in

[49] I 13, 1.   [51] I 14, 1.   [53] I 15, 1.
[50] I 13, 3.   [52] I 14, 10.   [54] I 15, 13.
[55] II 1, 1–II 5, 8. Winter is not again mentioned until II 10, 5; cf.
infra, pp. 63 f.
[56] *Supra*, p. 55.
[57] Theophyl. Sim. I 12, 12; Theophan. Conf., p. 253, 24; cf. *Chron. pasch.*,
p. 691.

the light of the above study of his terminology and method will be
seen to agree very readily with John of Ephesus and John of Biclar.
The conclusions arrived at therein show that the words "in this
current year" would in Theophylactus be used of a regnal year
only under the most exceptional circumstances. His customary
chronological unit is the year from spring to spring. He has already
marked the spring of 583 and his mention now of autumn indicates
clearly enough that he has made no departure from his normal
habit of thought. For this reason, it seems quite out of the question
that he would have intended the autumn of 584. To convey this
idea, he would have suddenly adopted the Emperor's year as the
basis of his chronology—something he does nowhere else. The only
exception to the rule is his statement that in the nineteenth year
of Maurice all was quiet in the Balkans and in the twentieth Peter
was appointed to the chief command.[58] This, however, is only an
apparent exception, because while he goes on to say that "in the
year before this"[59] Theodosius was married, he makes it clear that
the wedding took place in February.[60] Baynes thinks that Theophylactus has made an error here.[61] But he is quite capable of a
correct interpretation. By the nineteenth and twentieth years of
Maurice, he means not the regnal years August 14, 600-1 and
August 14, 601-2 respectively but the corresponding military years,
spring 601-2 and spring 602-3. When, therefore, he uses the words
"in the year before this," particularly since they follow immediately
his mention of the new appointment, he means only that Theodosius married during the winter previous to the opening of the
campaign season of 602. This view might seem, at first blush,
somewhat forced but it has in its favor that it gives Theophylactus
credit for an entirely consistent use of the word year. Moreover,
if by the words "in the year before this" Theophylactus actually
means the nineteenth regnal year of Maurice, i. e., February 601,
it is certainly peculiar that he never marks the transition back to the
twentieth year, but, after indicating winter as the time of Theo-

---

[58] VIII 4, 9.   [59] VIII 4, 10.
[60] VIII 4, 11. *Chron. pasch.*, p. 693, gives the same date for the marriage.
Theophan. Conf., pp. 283, 35–284, 1-3, places it by mistake in November
601.
[61] *Xénia*, p. 41, n. 2.

dosius' marriage, continues the narrative directly with a reference to the summer and autumn [62] of what is beyond any doubt Maurice's twentieth year, i. e., summer and autumn 602.[63] He is, then, quite well aware of the fact that the wedding took place in February 602, and the words " in the year before this " cannot be taken in a sense that is irreconcilable with the context.

To return now to the main point of the discussion, it is quite difficult to believe that by the words " in the current year," Theophylactus can mean the second year of Maurice; he must mean " in autumn of the year that ran from spring 583 to spring 584." Moreover, the same method of composition was followed here as that conjectured above with regard to the general summary.[64] It will be demonstrated in Part II of the present work that Theophylactus used John of Epiphania as the source for the Persian War. On the other hand, it has already been pointed out that he derived the miscellaneous items from a chronicle of Constantinople.[65] He first wrote an uninterrupted narrative of the Persian War. In this, the phrase " in the current year " was unequivocal. It was only later that he put in the notice about Maurice's consulship. He inserted it at this particular point because, just as in his mention of the eighth regnal year for the campaign of Bahram,[66] it was presumably a convenient device to indicate August 14, 583, without actual use of anything so unclassical as the Julian calendar; it has no more significance. Theophylactus was too good an historian not to feel cramped by the exigencies of his classicism, and not to realize that the usage of the chronicle had some advantages over the conventions that prevailed in the historiography of his day.

From the Battle of Solachon to the Mutiny. Solachon was fought in 585 and the mutiny began in 588. Theophylactus, however, between these events, records the passage of only two years, not three. Thus, after finishing his narrative of Solachon and its aftermath, he relates an invasion of Persia by Heraclius,[67] and only

---

[62] VIII 5, 5.

[63] With the mention of autumn of the same year (VIII 6, 2), Theophylactus begins the narrative of Maurice's downfall.

[64] *Supra,* pp. 59 f. [66] *Vide supra,* p. 58.

[65] *Supra,* p. 59. [67] II 10, 1-4.

then does he mark a new year by the mention of winter and spring.[68]
He here inserts a long account of the Avar Wars,[69] after which he
returns to the Persian front,[70] but he does not give another of his
characteristic references to the seasons until the winter before, and
the spring of, Philippicus' removal, i. e., 588.[71]

Obviously, the chronology is faulty. To remedy it, the mutiny
might, as Baynes suggests,[72] be stretched over two years, though
they would have to be 587 and 588, not 588 and 589; but, this puts
a rather forced interpretation on the sources. The evidence against
it has been gathered above and need not be repeated here.[73] De
Boor gives the key to a much better solution by pointing out a
lacuna in Theophylactus which occurs in the account preliminary
to Heraclius' invasion of Persia.[74] There is, of course, no way of
knowing just how much of the text has been lost, whether little or
great, but it appears not at all improbable that at least a reference
to the coming on of winter has dropped out. In the first place, one
of the mutilated sentences deals with Philippicus' measures to
strengthen the Roman fortifications in the Izala Mountains, a type
of work which would usually, though not always, be done in the
off season. Monocarton, for instance, had been repaired during
the winter.[75] Secondly, Philippicus' flight from Chlomaron took
place apparently late in the year.[76] On Honigmann's maps,[77]
Chlomaron is about fourteen miles due east of Martyropolis and
fully thirty-five miles southeast of Aphumon. Between Chlomaron
and Martyropolis flows the Nymphius. Aphumon is also on its
east bank. According to Theophylactus' account, Philippicus fled
panic-stricken from Chlomaron in the dead of night, seeking safety
blindly. He hurried off, however, not to the near-by Martyropolis
but to Aphumon.[78] He told no one of his design, but slipped away
in the deepest secrecy. The news spread swiftly through the camp.
The soldiers had no means of knowing what direction Philippicus
had taken nor why he had abandoned them. In the wildest con-

[68] II 10, 5 f.
[69] II 10, 8–II 17, 13.
[70] II 18, 1.
[71] II 18, 26; III 1, 3.
[72] *Op. cit.*, p. 37.
[73] *Vide supra*, p. 31.

[74] See his critical note to II 9, 17.
[75] *Supra*, p. 57.
[76] Theophyl. Sim. II 9, 1-16.
[77] *Ostgrenze d. byz. Reiches*, Map I.
[78] Theophyl. Sim. II 9, 4.

fusion of man and beast, they stumbled through the thick darkness. Yet, they too took the road to Aphumon.[79] The only explanation of this phenomenon is that the Nymphius barred the way to Marty-ropolis. The river, however was not always impassable. When on a previous occasion the Persians were besieging Aphumon, the Romans must have crossed far to the south.[80] In the flight from Chlomaron, therefore, the river was presumably swollen by the autumn rains.[81] In addition to this evidence that it was already late in the year, there is the whole tenor of Theophylactus' narra-tive. In 585, Philippicus received overtures from the Persians through Mebodes,[82] awaited a decision from Maurice,[83] fought the battle of Solachon,[84] devastated Arzanene thoroughly,[85] and laid siege for some time to Chlomaron.[86] Certainly, such movements must have pretty well taken up one military season. It is difficult to suppose that Heraclius could, over and above all these activities, have found time also for an invasion deep into Persian territory far to the south.[87] The chronology, therefore, that seems most likely is: 585, battle of Solachon, etc.; 586, Heraclius invades Persia; 587, reduces Persian fortresses; 588, Priscus appointed.

This concludes the positive discussion of the chronology; nega-tively, it still remains to solve the difficulties that can be raised against the above dates.

Chronology of Theophanes Confessor. This is as follows:

Sept. 582-83. John Mystacon appointed; fights battles on Nym-phius and at Acbas.[88]
Sept. 583-84. Philippicus appointed; invades territory of Nisibis.[89]
Sept. 584-85. Philippicus invades Arzanene; journeys to Con-stantinople.[90]

---

[79] *Ibid.*, II 9, 9.
[80] I 12, 1-7.
[81] Vital Cuinet, *La Turquie d'Asie. Géographie administrative, statis-tique, descriptive et raisonnée de chaque province de l'Asie-Mineure* (Paris 1890-94), II 415-16. He states that it seldom or never rains in this region between April and September.

[82] I 15, 1 ff.	[85] II 7, 1-5.	[88] P. 253, 14-22.
[83] I 15, 13.	[86] II 7, 6–II 9, 16.	[89] Pp. 253, 26-254, 3.
[84] I 15, 14–II 6, 13.	[87] II 10, 4.	[90] P. 254, 15-23.

Sept. 585-86. All events from battle of Solachon to Heraclius'
invasion of Persia.[91]

Sept. 586-87. All events from Heraclius' reduction of the Persian
fortresses through the history of the mutiny down
to the battle at Martyropolis in which Maruzas
was killed.[92]

Sept. 587-88. " In September of this year, the sixth indiction,
the Lombards began war on the Romans and the
Moorish tribes caused great confusion throughout
Africa." [93]

After this introductory notice are related the
escape of the prisoners captured at Dara and all
events through the invasion of Suania and the
revolt of Bahram down to the flight of Chosroes
and his arrival at Hierapolis.[94]

Sept. 588-89. Final defeat of Bahram and restoration of Chosroes.[95]

Adamek, in the work cited above,[96] demonstrates that the information on the Persian War in Theophanes comes entirely from Theophylactus,[97] but does not give their respective chronologies any
further consideration. This dependence, however, accounts entirely for the mistakes in Theophanes. He agrees with Theophylactus down to the appointment of Philippicus in the autumn of 583.
Here, however, he differs, placing the invasion of Arzanene not in
the spring of 584, but after September 584. The explanation is
quite simple. Theophylactus puts the invasion of Arzanene " in
the following year." [98] Theophanes understands the phrase not
of the following spring, which, as already proved,[99] was of course
meant, but takes it in his own sense of " year," the indiction year
that began in September. Accordingly, he dates it after the following September. Consistent thereafter, he brings the battle of
Solachon into 586. The chronology adopted in this dissertation
argues for a lacuna in the manuscripts of Theophylactus; but ap-

[91] Pp. 254, 27–256, 24.
[92] Pp. 259, 7–261, 13.   [96] *Supra*, p. 59.
[93] P. 261, 27-29.   [97] *Op. cit.*, pp. 25 f.
[94] Pp. 262, 2–265, 28.   [98] I 14, 1; *vide supra*, p. 61.
[95] Pp. 266, 13–267, 15.   [99] *Supra*, pp. 56 ff.

parently the text as it exists at present stood also before Theophanes, because he has Heraclius' invasion of Persia in the same year 586. For 587, therefore, the two authorities harmonize.[100]

Theophanes then does something rather astonishing. Instead of dating the mutiny in the following year, as plainly stated by his source,[101] he puts the whole rebellion in the same 587. Why? As proved by Adamek,[102] Theophanes made independent use of a local chronicle of Constantinople that Theophylactus had employed before him. But over and above this important fact, it can also be demonstrated that Theophanes not only drew his additional information from the document but even made it the basis of his chronology. Into the framework of the chronicle he forced the history of the Persian War. Theophylactus had launched his narrative of the momentous year in which Bahram revolted with a general summary of conditions throughout the Empire.[103] Herein he says: "In spring 589, old Rome was holding its own against the attacks of the Lombards while the strength of the Moors in Africa was continually growing weaker and, due to the multiplied victories of the Romans, they were sinking into an exhausted submissiveness." [104] The whole context shows that Theophylactus' point of view is not to give a synchronized history of warfare elsewhere, but merely to picture the actuality in the spring of 589. The very wording makes it obvious that he here describes not the beginning, but the end, of the incursions; the strength of the attack was already spent. But Theophanes in the chronicle that was his chronological guide found the entry that in September of the sixth indiction, i. e., September 587, the Lombards and Moors simultaneously renewed their warfare with the Empire.[105] What, then, did he do? Deceived by the superficial resemblance, he identified this item too hastily with the paragraph in Theophylactus. He took for granted that everything recorded before it in the historian had occurred previous to September 587 and arranged the material accordingly. Further indisputable evidence that this process

[100] It cannot, of course, be certain that Theophanes' copy of Theophylactus did not have a notice of time at this point, because the chronicler frequently disregards these indications.

[101] Theophyl. Sim. II 18, 26; III 1, 3.

[102] *Supra*, p. 59.   [103] *Supra*, p. 58.   [104] III 4, 8.   [105] P. 261, 27-29.

was followed is found in the fact that the escape of the prisoners taken at Dara is noted after September 587.[106] It came after the reference to Lombards and Moors in the historian; therefore, it occupies the same place in the chronicler. Yet, if there is one thing that Theophylactus makes painstakingly clear, it is that this feat happened, not in the spring of the year in which he tells it, but in the autumn of the previous year, and he goes to the great trouble of explicitly cautioning the reader against being deceived by its position in his narrative.[107] All this was lost on Theophanes, who quite ignores it, and it is obvious that for the chronology of the Persian War he has absolutely no authority.

Chronology of Bury and Baynes. Their chronology from 588 has already been discussed;[108] only their arrangement of events from 582 to 588 needs any attention here. It is as follows:

582. John Mystacon appointed; fights battle on Nymphius.[109]
583. John Mystacon fights battle at Acbas.
584. Philippicus appointed.
585. Philippicus invades Arzanene.[110]
586. Philippicus fights battle of Solachon; Heraclius invades Persia.[111]
587. Heraclius reduces the Persian fortresses.[112]
588. Priscus appointed; army mutinies.[113]

This chronology might be acceptable if Theophylactus were the sole source for the period from 582 to 588. As pointed out above,[114] he ordinarily does not date by regnal years, but his text, as it stands, offers some ground for presuming that he departed in one instance from his usual practice. If the " year " of Philippicus' appointment is Maurice's second year and not the military year, it is 584, not the autumn of 583.[115] If Theophylactus' statement can be interpreted in favor of 584, he then marks distinctly every year from

[106] Pp. 261, 29–262, 2.
[107] III 5, 8 and *vide supra*, pp. 59 f.
[108] *Supra*, esp. pp. 40. 52.
[109] Baynes, *Cambridge Medieval History*, II 277, n. 2; Bury, *Later Roman Empire*, II 105. Bury's 583 is merely an oversight.
[110] Bury, II 106.   [112] *Ibid.*, p. 108.   [114] *Supra*, p. 62.
[111] *Ibid.*   [113] *Ibid.*   [115] *Supra*, p. 61.

582 to 588; otherwise, he does not. But he is not the only source for the period. The Syriac John of Ephesus, a reliable writer contemporary with the event, puts the battle of Solachon in 585 and the Latin John of Biclar's vague notice supports him. Since, in addition, the normal interpretation of Theophylactus' narrative leads to the same conclusion, it is difficult to date the engagement in 586. If, as a consequence, he must be supposed to have over-looked one year, this constitutes no valid objection to the date 585. A lacuna occurs in the present text at the very point where a chronological notice might be expected and where the context leads the reader to anticipate it.

Chronology of Patrono.[116] This is as follows:

585. Philippicus invades Arzanene.[117]

586. Philippicus fights battle of Solachon.[117]

587. Priscus appointed; army mutinies.[118]

587-88 (Winter). Rebel army fights battle of Martyropolis in which Maruzas was killed.[119]

588. Escape of prisoners taken at Dara; [120] Philippicus recon-ciled with rebels; Martyropolis betrayed.[121]

590. Philippicus fights battle at Martyropolis against Mebodes and Aphraates; [122] Comentiolus appointed; wins victory at Nisibis; Bahram rebels.[123]

Patrono dates Solachon in 586 and follows Theophylactus in putting the appointment of Priscus at the return of the *second* spring thereafter.[124] Yet, he dates the appointment in 587, only one year later. He omits 589 altogether. Hence this chronology is untenable.[125]

---

[116] " Bizantini e Persiani alla fine del VI secolo," *Giornale della Società Asiatica Italiana* 20 (1907) 159-277.

[117] P. 211.

[118] P. 221.

[119] P. 225, n. 3.

[120] P. 226.

[121] Pp. 226-28.

[122] P. 228; cf. p. 216.

[123] P. 233.

[124] P. 217.

[125] These conclusions only confirm the judgment made long ago by E. Gerland in his review of the work; *vide BZ* 18 (1909) 569-71.

6

Chronology of Dölger's Regesten. Dölger dates the mutiny of the soldiers and the reconciliation with Philippicus in 587 and 588 respectively.[126] He thus prefers Patrono to Bury and Baynes. As it turns out, Bury and Baynes were better, but neither chronology was entirely correct. In the *Regesten,* therefore, all but one of the dates connected with the Persian War of Maurice will have to be corrected.

---

[126] P. 11, Nrs. 88-91.

SUMMARY

The discussion in Chapter I has led to conclusions which are, at least in the eyes of the author, the most important results of the dissertation. In the first place, the determination of the dates at which the month was intercalated in the Persian religious calendar and the demonstration that the epagomenae were omitted in 590, make it possible now to calculate any date of the Persian civil or religious year in terms of the Julian calendar. Secondly, the solution of the chronological problem presented by the Syriac Acts of the Persian Martyrs provides a new basis for a critical examination of these significant hagiographical documents. Thirdly, light has been cast on the most obscure portions of Sassanid chronology. It has been established that the first year of Bahram I began on September 19, 272 and that Sapor I was probably crowned on March 1, 240. Equally interesting and important are the fixing of the date of Mani's death, February 24, 273, and the explanation for the long-standing puzzle of the beginning of the Armenian Era.

In Chapters II, III, and IV, a solution is offered for the chronological difficulties of the Persian War of the Emperor Maurice. It has the advantage of reconciling the Oriental with the Greek sources. The Persian and Arabic authorities who depend on the *Khvadhay-namagh* (Persian Royal Annals) have been, as a rule, somewhat slighted by Byzantine scholars. This attitude goes back to Nöldeke. Since he put the accession of Chosroes II too late in the year, he felt compelled to reject much of the information found in the Oriental writers. Their right to greater consideration, however, is vindicated by the results of the present work. The details of the chronology worked out in Chapters II, III, and IV are summarized in the following table:

72   *The Persian War of the Emperor Maurice*

CHRONOLOGICAL TABLE OF THE PERSIAN WAR
OF THE EMPEROR MAURICE

Dölger's *Regesten*		
	582	After Aug. 14. John Mystacon appointed.
		Autumn. John Mystacon fights battle on Nymphius.
	583	April. (Fire in Forum at Constantinople.)
		Before May 10. John Mystacon fights battle at Acbas.
		May 10. (Earthquake at Constantinople.)
		After Aug. 14. Philippicus appointed.
		Autumn. Philippicus invades territory of Nisibis twice.
		Winter. Philippicus repairs Monocarton.
	584	Spring. Philippicus invades Arzanene.
		Spring. Philippicus falls ill.
		Winter. Philippicus journeys to Constantinople.
586 Spring-Summer	585	Spring. Philippicus rejects, at Maurice's orders, peace offered through Mebodes.[1]
		Summer. Philippicus fights battle of Solachon.
		Summer. Aphraates marzban of Armenia.
		Summer. Philippicus invades Arzanene.
		Autumn. Philippicus besieges Chlomaron.
	586	Heraclius invades Persia.
	587	Heraclius reduces Persian fortresses.
587 Before Mar. 30	588	Before Apr. 18. Maurice lowers the pay of the army.
		Before Apr. 18. Priscus appointed.
		Apr. 21. Army mutinies.
		Before July 1. Army elects rival emperor.
		Before July 1. Army rejects Philippicus.
587 About Summer		Summer. Army invades Persia; fights at Calkadzhur; receives Aristobulus.
		July-Aug. Bahram defeats the Turks.
		Autumn. Army (mutinous) invades Persia a second time.
		Autumn. Army (mutinous) fights battle at Martyropolis in which Maruzas was killed.
		Autumn. Escape of prisoners taken at Dara.
		Oct. 29. Earthquake at Antioch.
	589	Spring. "Chazars" invade Azerbaijan.
588 Before Apr. 12		Before Apr. 4. Maurice's letter to Gregory of Antioch.

---

[1] Mebodes' embassy took place before the battle of Solachon; cf. *supra*, p. 65.

588 Before Apr. 12	Apr. 4. Army reconciled by Gregory.
	Apr. 8. Bahram returns to Rai after victory over Turks.
	After Apr. 4. Maurice's letter to Philippicus.[2]
	Middle of May. Martyropolis betrayed to Persians.
	Middle of May. Aphraates dispatched to Martyropolis.
	Middle of May. Bahram ordered into Suania.
590 (About)	Spring and Summer. Revolt of Smbat Bagratuni in Armenia.
	About July 1. Philippicus battles Mebodes and Aphraates at Martyropolis.
	After July. Comentiolus succeeds Philippicus.
	After Aug. Bahram defeated in Albania.
	After Aug. 14. Bahram revolts against Hormisdas.
	Autumn. John Mystacon besieges Dvin.
	Before Nov. 1. Bahram arrives near Mosul.
	Before Nov. 1. Comentiolus wins victory of Nisibis; death of Aphraates.
	Before Winter. Comentiolus captures Acbas.
590	Feb. 6. Hormisdas IV deposed.
	Feb. 15. Chosroes II crowned.
	Feb. 20. Bahram arrives at Naharwan.
	Feb. 28. Bahram defeats Chosroes.
	Mar. 9. Bahram crowned.
	March. Chosroes reaches Hierapolis.
591 Spring	March. Maurice orders Comentiolus to receive Chosroes.
" "	Later. Maurice orders Chosroes to remain in Hierapolis.
" "	Late Autumn. Maurice officially promises aid to Chosroes.
" "	Late Autumn. Maurice orders Dometianus and Gregory to accompany Chosroes.
" "	Late Autumn. Maurice orders John Mystacon to support Bindoes.
591	Jan. 7. Rosas begins expedition against Zadespras.
	Feb. 9. Chosroes receives head of Zadespras.
	Feb. 16(?). Chosroes surrenders Martyropolis.
" "	Spring. Maurice makes formal treaty with Chosroes (Theophyl. Sim. V 2, 4–V 3, 1).
	Before Oct. 1. Chosroes finally defeats Bahram.

[2] Theophylactus and Evagrius do not say very definitely whether Maurice wrote the letter before Gregory's negotiations with the mutinous army or after. Their language, however, implies that it was after; cf. *supra*, p. 33.

LIST OF SOURCES AND WORKS CITED

A. SOURCES

Agapius of Hierapolis. *Kitab al-Unvan. Histoire universelle écrite par Agapius (Mahboub) de Menbidj, éditée et traduite en français par* A. Vasiliev, PO V 559-692; VII 457-592; VIII 397-550, XI 1-144, Paris 1910-15.

Albiruni. *The Chronology of Ancient Nations, an English Version of the Arabic Text of the Athar-ul-Bakuja of Albiruni, or, " Vestiges of the Past," Collected and Reduced to Writing by the Author in A. H. 390-391, A. D. 1000, Translated and Edited, with Notes and Index by* E. Sachau, Oriental Translation Fund of Great Britain and Ireland, London 1879.

Anonymous of Fourmont. M. l'Abbé Fourmont, *Histoire d'une révolution arrivée en Perse dans le sixième siècle,* Histoire de l'Académie Royale des Inscriptions et Belles Lettres, avec les Mémoires de Littérature tirez des Registres de cette Académie, depuis l'année M.DCCXXVI jusques et compris l'année M.DCCXXX, VII (Paris 1733) 325-33. Cf. *Preface,* p. viii.

Anonymous of 724. *Chronicon miscellaneum ad annum domini 724 pertinens interpretatus est* J.-B. Chabot, CSCO, scriptores Syri, III 4, Chronica minora, Paris and Leipzig 1904.

Anonymus Guidi. *Chronicon anonymum interpretatus est* I. Guidi, CSCO, scriptores Syri, III 4, Chronica minora, Paris and Leipzig 1903.

Bar-Hebraeus. *Gregorii Barhebraei chronicon ecclesiasticum quod e codice Musei Britannici descriptum conjuncta opera ediderunt, latinitate donarunt annotationibusque theologicis, historicis, geographicis et archaeologicis illustrarunt* J.-B. Abbeloos et T. J. Lamy, 3 vols., Paris and Louvain 1872-77.

————. *The Chronography of Gregory Abul Faraj the Son of Aaron, the Hebrew Physician, Commonly Known as Bar Hebraeus, being the First Part of His Political History of the World, Translated from the Syriac by* E. A. Wallis Budge, 2 vols., Oxford and London 1932.

Belami. *Chronique de Abou-Djafar-Mohammed-ben-Djarir-ben-Yezid Tabari, traduite sur la version persane d'Abou-Ali-Mohammed Belami, d'après les manuscrits de Paris, de Gotha, de Londres et de Canterbury par* H. Zotenberg, Oriental Translation Fund of Great Britain and Ireland, 4 vols., Paris 1867-74.

Chronicon paschale. *Chronicon paschale ad exemplar Vaticanum recensuit* L. Dindorf, Corpus Scriptorum Historiae Byzantinae, Bonn 1832.

Chronicon Seert. *Histoire nestorienne (Chronique de Séert) publiée et traduite par* Mgr. A. Scher, PO IV 213-313; V 217-344; VII 93-203; XIII 433-639 (*Avec le concours de* Robert Griveau), Paris 1908-19. (ChrS.)

75

76   The Persian War of the Emperor Maurice

Dinawari. *Abu Hanifa ad-Dinaweri. Kitab al-akhbar at-tiwal publié par* V. Guirgass, Leiden 1888. The author used this work in a translation made for him by Rev. Edw. P. Arbez.

Elias of Nisibis. *Eliae metropolitae Nisibeni opus chronologicum interpretatus est* E. W. Brooks, CSCO, scriptores Syri, III 7, Rome, Paris, and Leipzig 1910.

Eutychius. *Contextio gemmarum, sive Eutychii patriarchae Alexandrini annales, interprete* E. Pocock, MPG, 57, 525-792.

Evagrius. *The Ecclesiastical History of Evagrius with the Scholia, Edited with Introduction, Critical Notes, and Indices by* J. Bidez and L. Parmentier, Methuen's Byzantine Texts edited by J. B. Bury, London 1898.

————. *Evagrii scholastici Epiphaniensis et ex praefectis ecclesiasticae historiae libri sex, interprete* H. Valois, MPG, 86², 2406-2906.

Firdausi. *The Shah Nameh: An Heroic Poem, Containing the History of Persia from Kioomurs to Yesdejird; that is, from the Earliest Times to the Conquest of that Empire by the Arabs, by Abool Kasim Firdousee; Carefully Collated with a Number of the Oldest and Best Manuscripts, and Illustrated by a Copious Glossary of Obsolete Words and Obscure Idioms; with an Introduction and Life of the Author in English and Persian; and an Appendix, Containing the Interpolated Episodes, etc. Found in Different Manuscripts by* T. Macan, 4 vols., Calcutta 1829.

————. *Le livre des rois par Aboulkasim Firdousi traduit et commenté par* J. Mohl, 7 vols., Paris 1876-78.

————. *The Shahnama of Firdausi Done into English by* A. G. Warner and E. Warner, 9 vols., London 1905-25.

Gregory the Great. *Gregorii I Papae registrum epistolarum ed.* P. Ewald and L. M. Hartmann, MGH, epistolarum I-II, 2 vols., Berlin 1887-99.

Histoire de la Géorgie. M. Brosset, *Histoire de la Géorgie depuis l'antiquité jusqu'au XIXᵉ siècle traduite du géorgien. 1ʳᵉ partie, histoire ancienne, jusqu'au 1469 de J.-C.*, St. Petersburg 1849-50. *Additions et éclaircissements*, St. Petersburg 1851.

James of Edessa. *Chronicon Jacobi Edesseni interpretatus est* E. W. Brooks, CSCO, scriptores Syri, III 4, Chronica minora, Paris and Leipzig 1905.

John of Biclar. *Iohannis abbatis monasterii Biclarensis chronica edidit* Th. Mommsen, MGH, auctores antiquissimi, XI, Chronica minora, II, Berlin 1894.

John of Ephesus. *Die Kirchengeschichte des Johannes v. Ephesus aus dem Syrischen übersetzt, mit einer Abhandlung über die Tritheiten von* J. M. Schönfelder, Munich 1862.

John of Nikiu. *The Chronicle of John, Bishop of Nikiu, Translated from Zotenberg's Ethiopic Text by* R. H. Charles, Text and Translation Society, London and Oxford 1916.

Manichaean Documents. A von le Coq, *Türkische Manichaica aus Chotscho,* Abhandlungen der preussischen Akademie der Wissenschaften, philosophisch-historische Classe, Anhang, Abh. VI, Berlin 1911.

———. F. C. Andreas (†)—W. Henning, "Mitteliranische Manichaica aus Chinesisch-Turkestan III. von F. C. Andreas (†), aus dem Nachlass herausgegeben," *Sitzungsberichte der preussischen Akademie der Wissenschaften, philosophisch-historische Klasse* (1934), pp. 848-912.

al-Maqdisi. *Le livre de la création et de l'histoire de Motahhar ben Tahir el-Maqdisi attribué à Abou-Zeid Ahmed ben Sahl el-Balkhi publié et traduit d'après le manuscrit de Constantinople par* Cl. Huart, Publications de l'École des Langues Orientales Vivantes, 6 vols., Paris 1899-1919.

Masudi. *Maçoudi. Les prairies d'or, texte et traduction par* C. Barbier de Meynard et Pavet de Courteille, Collection d'ouvrages orientaux publiée par la Société Asiatique, 9 vols., Paris 1861-77.

Menander Protector. *Excerpta historica iussu imp. Constantini Porphyrogeniti confecta ediderunt* U. Ph. Boissevain, C. de Boor, Th. Büttner-Wobst, 4 vols. in 6, Berlin 1903-10.

Michael Syrus. *Chronique de Michel le Syrien, patriarche jacobite d'Antioche (1166-1199), éditée pour la première fois et traduite en français par* J.-B. Chabot, 4 vols., Paris 1899-1924.

Mirkhond. A. I. Silvestre de Sacy, *Mémoires sur diverses antiquités de la Perse, et sur les médailles des rois de la dynastie des Sassanides; suivis de l'histoire de cette dynastie, traduite du persan de Mirkhond,* Paris 1793.

Nicephorus Callistus Xanthopulus. *Nicephori Callisti Xanthopuli ecclesiasticae historiae libri xviii,* MPG, 145-47.

Nihayat. E. G. Browne, "Some Account of the Arabic Work Entitled 'Nihayatu'l-irab fi akhbari'l-Fars wa'l-Arab,' Particularly of that Part which Treats of the Persian Kings," *Journal of the Royal Asiatic Society of Great Britain and Ireland,* 1900, pp. 195-259.

Pseudo-Sebeos. F. Macler. "Pseudo-Sebêos, texte arménien traduit et annoté," *Journal Asiatique*[10], 6 (1905) 121-56.

Ibn Qutaiba. *Ibn Coteiba's Handbuch der Geschichte, aus den Handschriften der k. k. Hofbibliothek zu Wien, der herzoglichen Bibliothek zu Gotha und der Universitäts-Bibliothek zu Leyden, herausgegeben von* F. Wüstenfeld, Göttingen 1850. The author used this work in the translation of Rev. Edw. P. Arbez.

Sebeos. *Histoire d'Héraclius par l'Évêque Sebêos traduite de l'arménien et annotée par* F. Macler, Paris 1904.

Stephen of Taron. *Des Stephanos von Taron armenische Geschichte aus dem Altarmenischen übersetzt von* H. Gelzer and A. Burckhardt, Scriptores sacri et profani, fasc. iv, Leipzig 1907.

Syriac Acts of the Persian Martyrs. O. Braun, *Ausgewählte Akten per-*

sischer Märtyrer (mit einem Anhang: ostsyrisches Mönchsleben) aus dem Syrischen übersetzt, Bibliothek der Kirchenväter, Kempten and Munich 1915.

——. G. Hoffmann, *Auszüge aus syrischen Akten persischer Märtyrer übersetzt und durch Untersuchungen zur historischen Topographie erläutert,* Abhandlungen für die Kunde des Morgenlandes herausgegeben von der Deutschen Morgenländischen Gesellschaft, VII 3, Leipzig 1880.

Tabari. *Geschichte der Perser und Araber zur Zeit der Sasaniden, aus der arabischen Chronik des Tabari übersetzt und mit ausführlichen Erläuterungen und Ergänzungen versehn von* Th. Nöldeke, Leiden 1879.

al-Thaalibi. *Histoire des rois des Perses par Abu Mansur Abd al-Malik ibn Mohammed ibn Ismail al-Thaalibi, texte arabe publié et traduit par* H. Zotenberg, Paris 1900.

Theophanes Confessor. *Theophanis Chronographia* ed. by C. de Boor, 2 vols., Leipzig 1883-85.

Theophylactus Simocatta. *Theophylacti Simocattae historiae* ed. by C. de Boor, Leipzig 1887.

Thomas Ardzruni. M. Brosset, *Collection d'historiens arméniens traduits,* 2 vols., St. Petersburg 1874-76.

Thomas of Marga. *The Book of Governors: The Historia Monastica of Thomas, Bishop of Marga, A. D. 840, Edited from Syriac Manuscripts in the British Museum and Other Libraries by* E. A. Wallis Budge, 2 vols., London 1893.

al-Yaqubi. *Ibn-Wadhih qui dicitur al-Jaqubi historiae—Pars prior historiam ante-Islamicam continens edidit indicesque adjecit* M. Th. Houtsma, 2 vols., Leiden 1883. The author used this work in the translation of Rev. Edw. P. Arbez.

B. MODERN WORKS

Adamek, O., *Beiträge zur Geschichte des byzantinischen Kaisers Mauricius (582-602),* Jahresbericht des ersten k. k. Staats-Gymnasiums in Graz, 2 parts, Graz 1890-91.

Allen, W. E. D., *A History of the Georgian People,* London 1932.

Andreas (†), F. C., See *Sources, Manichaean Documents.*

Assemani, J. S., *Bibliotheca orientalis Clementino-Vaticana,* 3 vols. in 4, Rome 1719-28.

Baumstark, A., *Geschichte der syrischen Literatur mit Ausschluss der christlich-palästinensischen Texte,* Bonn 1922.

Baynes, N. H., *The Literary Construction of the History of Theophylactus Simocatta,* Xénia, hommage international à l'Université Nationale de Grèce à l'occasion du soixante-quinzième anniversaire de sa fondation (1837-1912), Athens 1912.

Braun, O., See *Sources, Syriac Acts of Persian Martyrs.*

Brosset, M., See *Sources, Histoire de la Géorgie.*

Bury, J. B., "The Chronology of Theophylaktos Simokatta," *English Historical Review,* 3 (1888) 310-15.

———, *A History of the Later Roman Empire from Arcadius to Irene (395 A.D. to 800 A.D.),* 2 vols., London and New York 1889.

Cambridge Medieval History. Planned by J. B. Bury. Edited by H. M. Gwatkin, J. P. Whitney, J. R. Tanner, C. W. Previté-Orton, and Z. N. Brooke, 8 vols., New York and Cambridge, England 1913-36.

Christensen, A., *L'Iran sous les Sassanides,* Copenhagen 1936.

———, *Les types du premier homme et du premier roi dans l'histoire légendaire des Iraniens,* Archives d'études orientales publiées par J.-A. Lundell, 14, 2 vols., Stockholm and Leiden 1917-34.

Clemen, C., *Mazdaismus,* RE, Suppl.-Band V 679-704.

Coq, A. von le, See *Sources, Manichaean Documents.*

CSCO. Corpus Scriptorum Christianorum Orientalium, Rome, Paris, and Leipzig 1903 ff.

Cuinet, V., *La Turquie d'Asie. Géographie administrative, statistique, descriptive et raisonnée de chaque province de l'Asie-Mineure,* 4 vols., Paris 1890-94.

Delehaye, H., S. J., *Synaxarium Ecclesiae Constantinopolitanae e codice Sirmondiano nunc Berolinensi adiectis synaxariis selectis,* Propylaeum ad Acta Sanctorum Novembris, Brussels 1902.

Dölger, Fr., *Regesten der Kaiserurkunden des oströmischen Reiches von 565-1453,* Corpus der griechischen Urkunden des Mittelalters und der neueren Zeit, Reihe A, Regesten, 2 parts, Munich and Berlin 1924.

Ensslin, W., *Mauricius,* RE 14, 2387-93.

Exc. Const. See *Sources, Menander.*

Gerland, E., "C. M. Patrono, Bizantini e Persiani alla fine del VI secolo," *Byzantinische Zeitschrift,* 18 (1909) 569-71.

———, "Erich Merten. Zum Perserkriege der byzantinischen Kaiser Justinos II. und Tiberios II. (571-579 nach Chr.)," *Berliner Philologische Wochenschrift,* 33 (1913) 48-49.

Ginzel, F. K., *Handbuch der mathematischen und technischen Chronologie,* 3 vols., Leipzig 1906-14.

Grundriss der iranischen Philologie, ed. by W. Geiger and E. Kuhn, Strasbourg 1895 ff.

Gutschmid, A. von, "Über das iranische Jahr," *Berichte über die Verhandlungen der königlich sächsischen Gesellschaft der Wissenschaften zu Leipzig, philologisch-historische Classe,* 14 (1862) 1-9.

Henning, W., See *Sources, Manichaean Documents.*

Hoffmann, Georg, See *Sources, Syriac Acts of Persian Martyrs.*

Honigmann, E., *Die Ostgrenze des byzantinischen Reiches von 363 bis 1071 nach griechischen, arabischen, syrischen und armenischen Quellen,* Corpus Bruxellense Historiae Byzantinae, Nr. 3, Brussels 1935.

80   *The Persian War of the Emperor Maurice*

Hübschmann, H., "Die altarmenischen Ortsnamen mit Beiträgen zur historischen Topographie Armeniens und einer Karte," *Indogermanische Forschungen*, 16 (1904) 197-490.

Kmosko, M., S. *Simeon bar Sabbae praefatus est, textum Syriacum vocalium signis instruxit, latine vertit, notis illustravit*, Patrologia Syriaca, II (Paris 1907) 659-1054.

Labourt, J., *Le Christianisme dans l'Empire Perse sous la dynastie sassanide (224-632)*, Bibliothèque de l'enseignement de l'histoire ecclésiastique, 2nd ed., Paris 1904.

Lietzmann, D. Hans, *Zeitrechnung der römischen Kaiserzeit, des Mittelalters und der Neuzeit für die Jahre 1-2000 nach Christus*, Sammlung Göschen Nr. 1085, Berlin and Leipzig 1934.

Lynch, H. F. B., *Armenia. Travels and Studies*, 2 vols., London, New York, and Bombay 1901.

MGH. Monumenta Germaniae Historica.

MPG. Migne, Patrologia Graeca.

Dr. *Modi Memorial Volume. Papers on Indo-Iranian Subjects, Written by Several Scholars, in Honour of Shams-ul-Ulama Dr. Jivanji Jamshedji Modi, B.A., Ph.D., C.I.E., J.P.*, Bombay 1930.

Mordtmann, A. D., "Die Chronologie der Sassaniden," *Sitzungsberichte der philosophisch-philologischen Classe der k. b. Akademie der Wissenschaften zu München*, 1 (1871) 3-30.

———, "Hekatompylos. Ein Beitrag zur vergleichenden Geographie Persiens," *Sitzungsberichte der k. b. Akademie· der Wissenschaften zu München*, 1869[1], pp. 497-536.

Nöldeke, Tab. See *Sources, Tabari*.

Patkanian, M. K., See below, *Prud'homme*.

Patrono, C. M., "Bizantini e Persiani alla fine del VI secolo," *Giornale della Società Asiatica Italiana*, 20 (1907) 159-277.

PO. Patrologia Orientalis, ed. by R. Graffin and F. Nau, Paris 1907 ff.

Prud'homme, É., "Essai d'une histoire de la dynastie des Sassanides d'après les renseignements fournis par les historiens arméniens, par M. K. Patkanian: traduit du russe," *Journal Asiatique*[6], 7 (1866) 101-238.

Ramsay, A. M., "The Speed of the Roman Imperial Post,"·*Journal of Roman Studies*, 15 (1925) 60-74.

Rawlinson, H. C., "Notes on a Journey to Tabriz, through Persian Kurdistan, to the Ruins of Takhti-Soleiman, and from Thence by Zanjan and Tarom, to Gilan, in October· and November 1838," *Journal of the Royal Geographical·Society of London*, 10 (1841) 1-64.

RE. Pauly's Real-Encyclopädie der classischen Altertumswissenschaft, neue Bearbeitung begonnen von Georg Wissowa unter Mitwirkung zahlreicher Fachgenossen herausgegeben von Wilhelm Kroll und Karl Mittelhaus, Stuttgart 1894 ff.

Schaeder, H. H., "Carl Schmidt und H. J. Polotsky: Ein Mani-Fund aus Ägypten. Originalschriften des Mani und seiner Schüler. Mit einem Beitrag von H. Ibscher," *Gnomon*. 9 (1933) 337-62.

Schaeder, H. H., *Iranica*, Abhandlungen der Gesellschaft der Wissenschaften
    zu Göttingen, philologisch-historische Klasse, III 10, Göttingen 1934.
Stein, E., *Studien zur Geschichte des byzantinischen Reiches vornehmlich
    unter den Kaisern Justinus II u. Tiberius Constantinus*, Stuttgart
    1919.
Stieler's Atlas of Modern Geography, 10th ed., completely revised and
    largely redrawn under the direction of Professor Dr. H. Haack, 2
    vols., Gotha 1930-31.
Taqizadeh, S. H., " Some Chronological Data relating to the Sasanian
    Period," *Bulletin of the School of Oriental Studies (University of
    London)*, 9 (1937) 125-39.
Wright, W., *Catalogue of the Syriac Manuscripts in the British Museum,
    Acquired Since the Year 1838*, 3 vols., London 1870-72.

INDEX

CPSIA information can be obtained
at www.ICGtesting.com
Printed in the USA
BVHW052336060223
658028BV00008B/281

9 781013 6096